Copyright © 2022 by
Sweet Ollie Learning

All Rights Reserved.

No part of this book may be used or reproduced by any means, graphic, electronic, or mechanical, including photocopying, recording, taping, or by any information storage retrieval system without the written permission of the publisher except in the case of brief quotations embodied in critical articles and reviews.

Playful Publishing LLC
www.playfulpublishingllc.com

Children's Learning Activity Book
for Kids 3-6 (color interior)
ISBN 978-1-959236-53-5

This Book Belongs to

_____

_____

Contents

- Shape and Color Recognition
- Alphabet Tracing
- Number Tracing
- Shape Tracing
- Cut and Paste
- Line Tracing
- Symmetry
- Matching
- Patterns
- Mazes
- Math

Let's Get Started!

Dinosaur Tracing

Help these dinosaurs find their way to their leafy snack!

Which One is Different?
Circle the different flower in each group!

SMALLEST

Circle the smallest object in each row.

My 5 Senses

Trace the word and colour the picture.

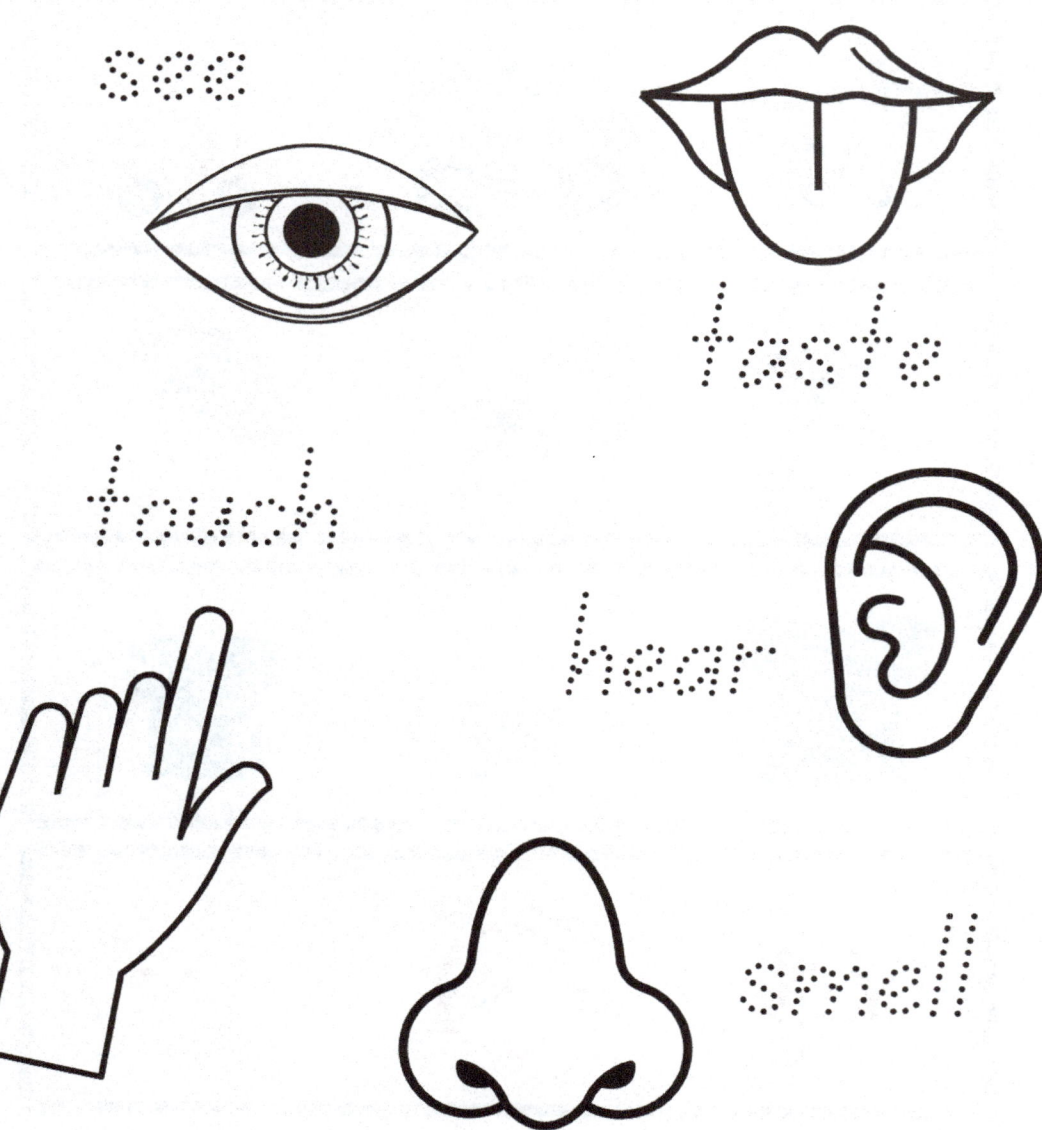

- Match the same colors.

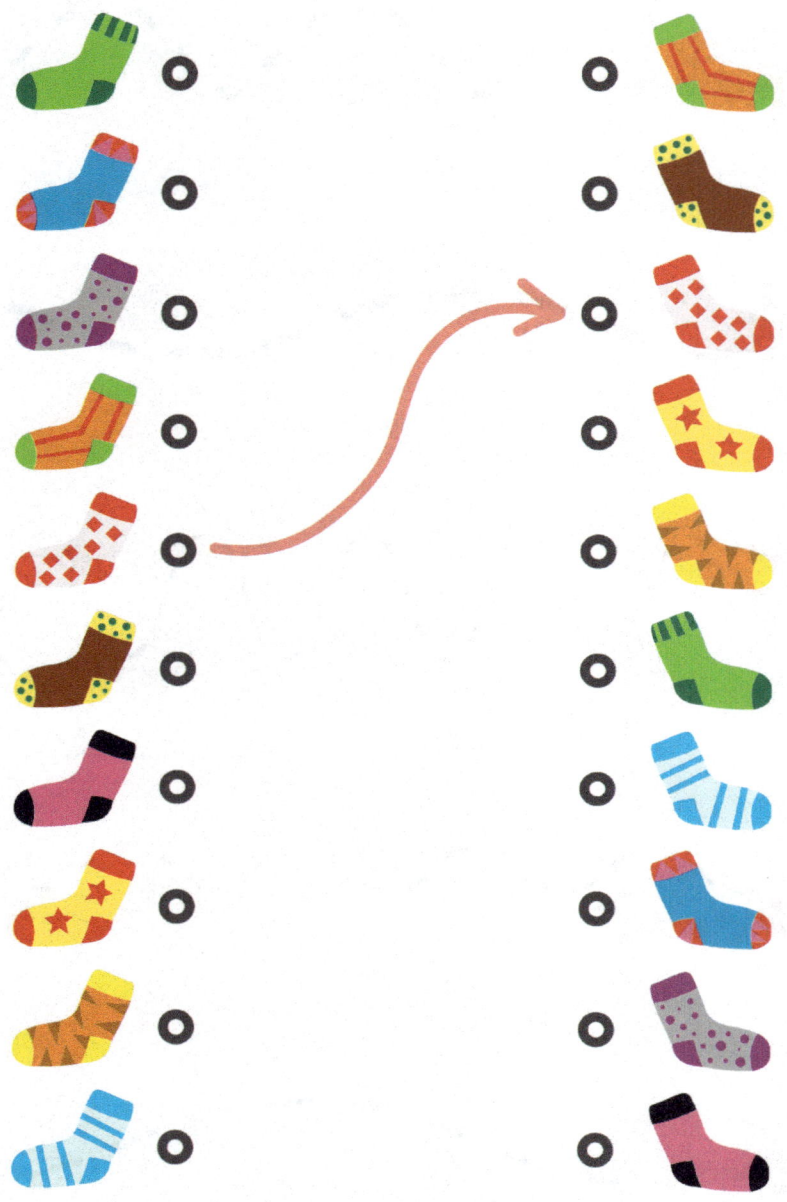

CAN YOU DO IT?

Directions: Read the questions and circle your answer.

Can you ride a bicycle?

| Yes, I can. | No, I can't. |

Can you climb a tree?

| Yes, I can. | No, I can't. |

Can you swim?

| Yes, I can. | No, I can't. |

Can you sing a song?

| Yes, I can. | No, I can't. |

Can you dance?

| Yes, I can. | No, I can't. |

SYMMETRY

Trace and color to make a symmetrical boat:

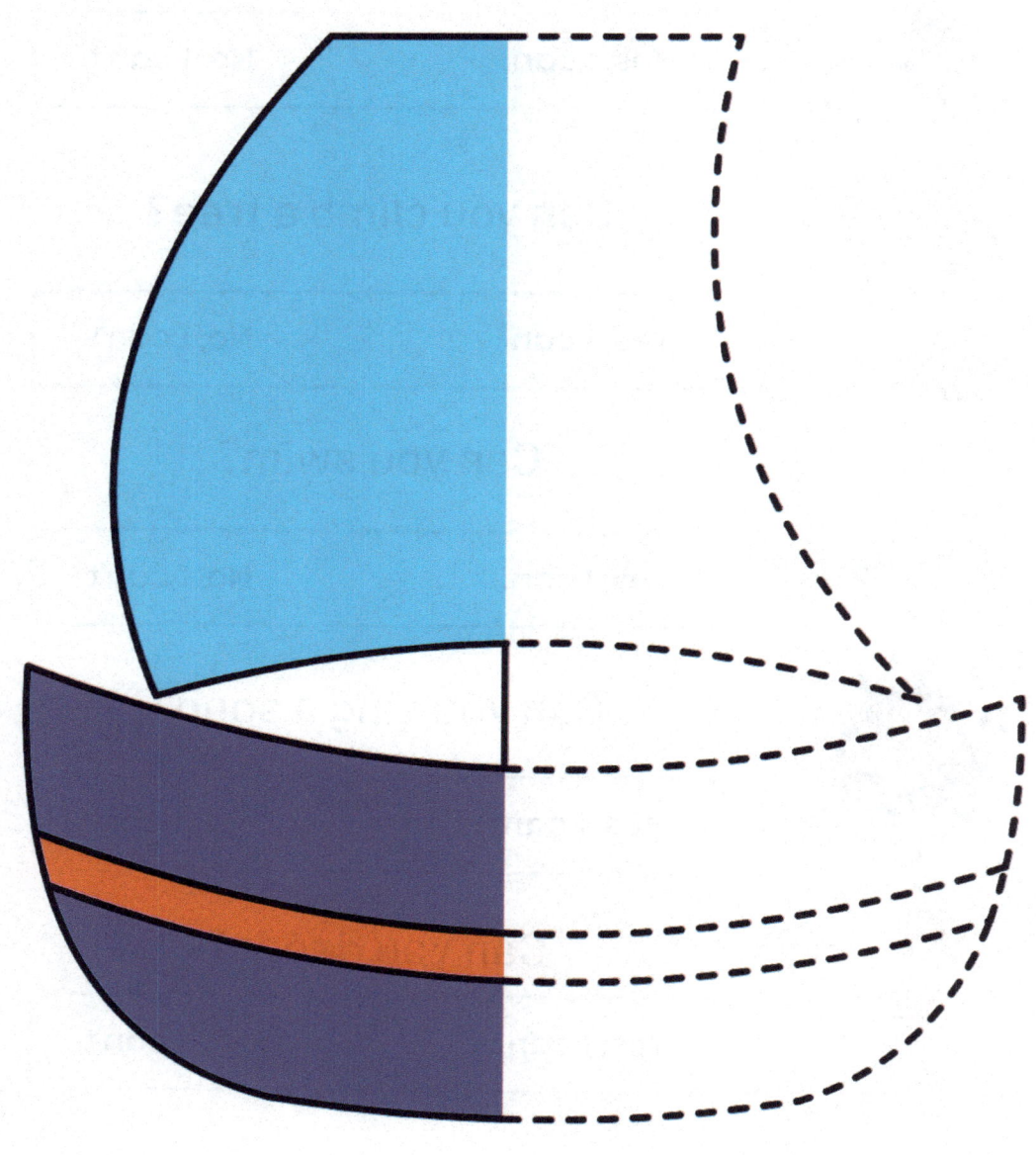

Tracing Shapes

Square

Circle

Hexagon

Rectangle

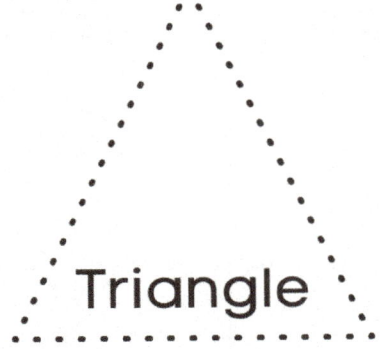

Triangle

Star

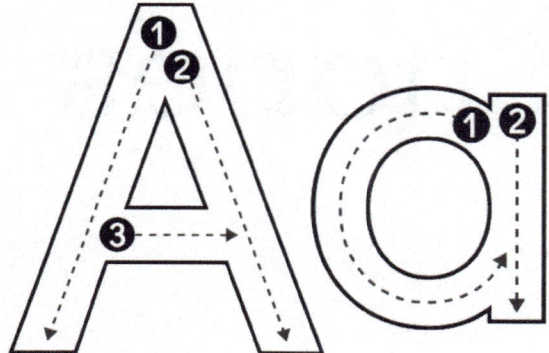 A is for

Apple

Ant

Anchor

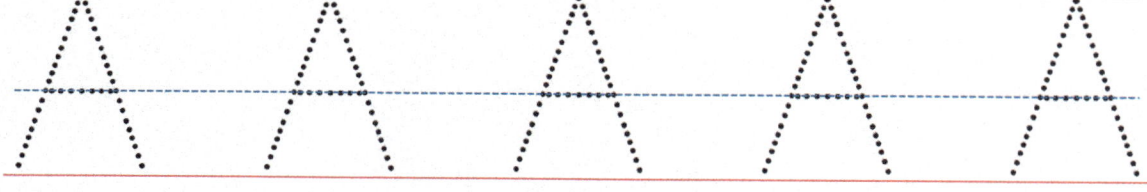

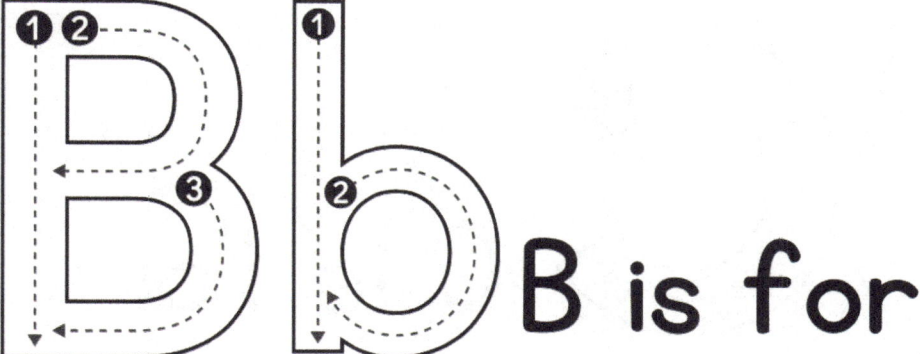

B is for

Banana Ball Butterfly

Cc C is for

Carrot   Cake   Cat

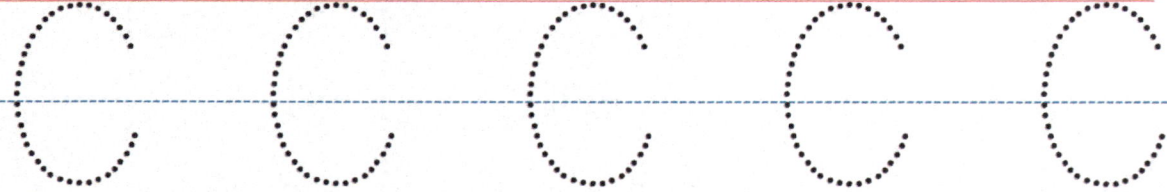

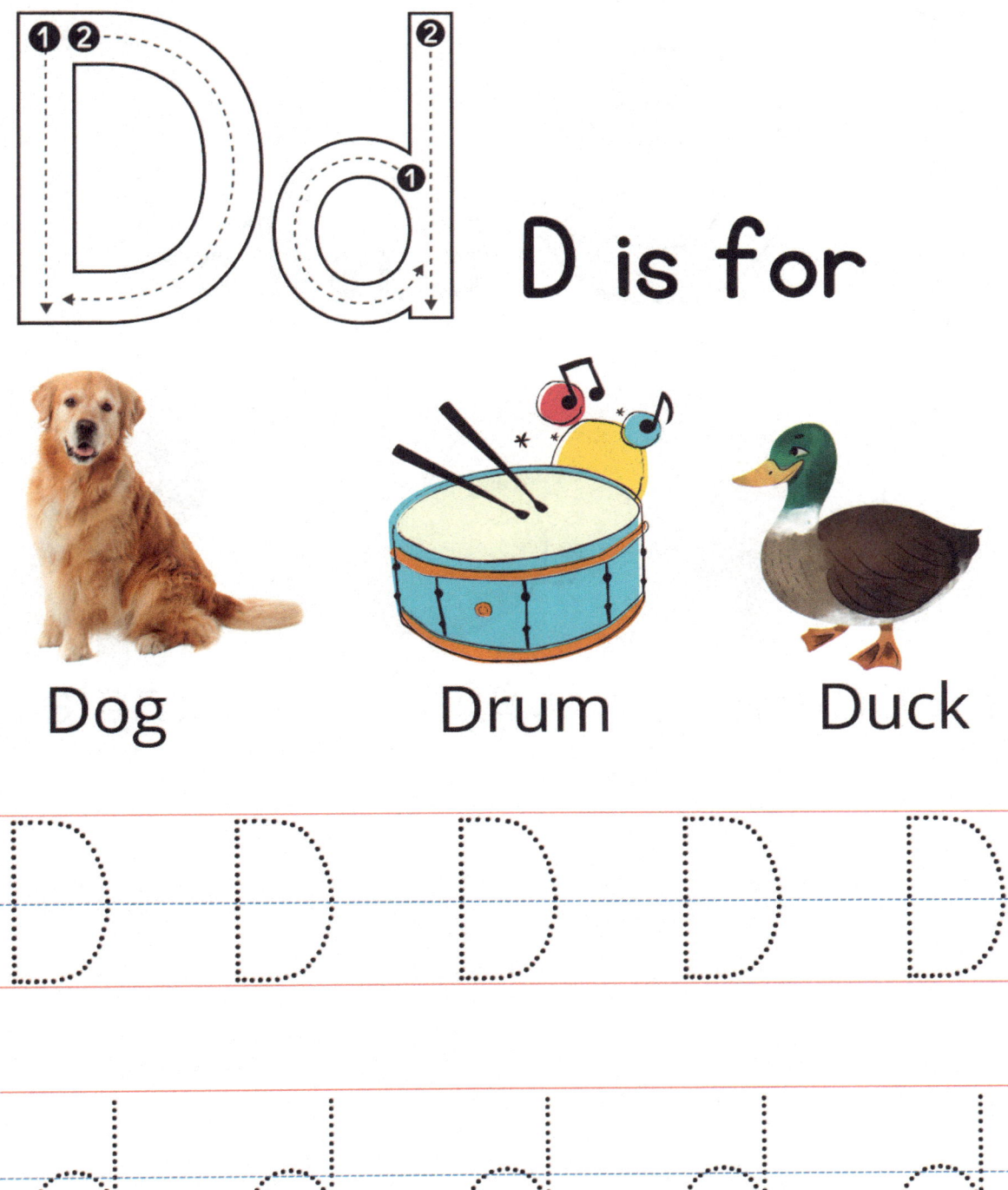

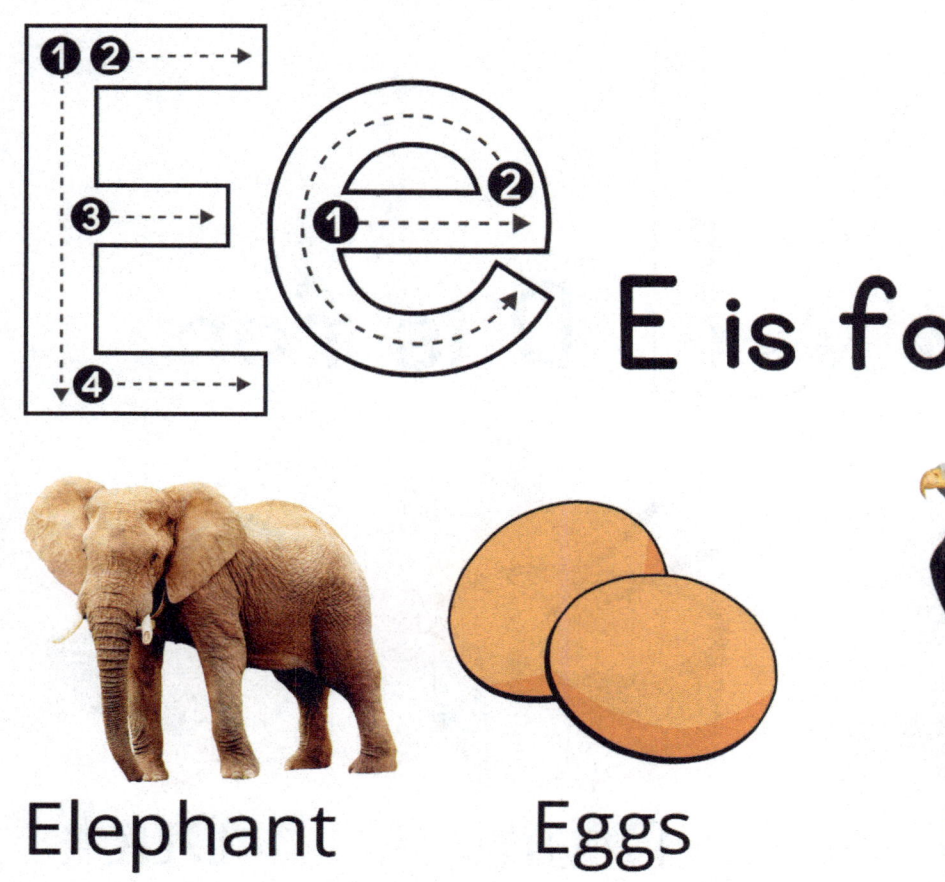

E is for

Elephant   Eggs    Eagle

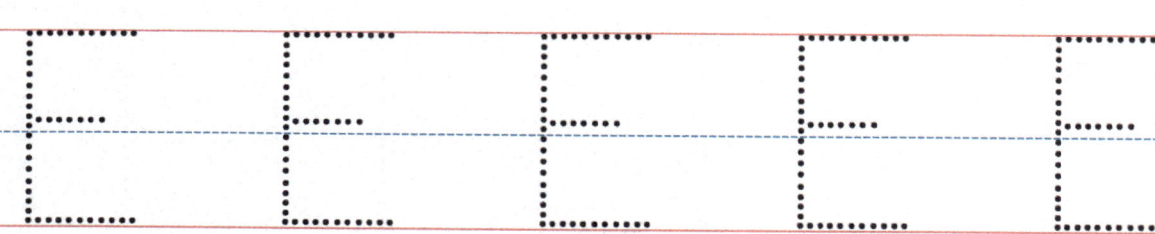

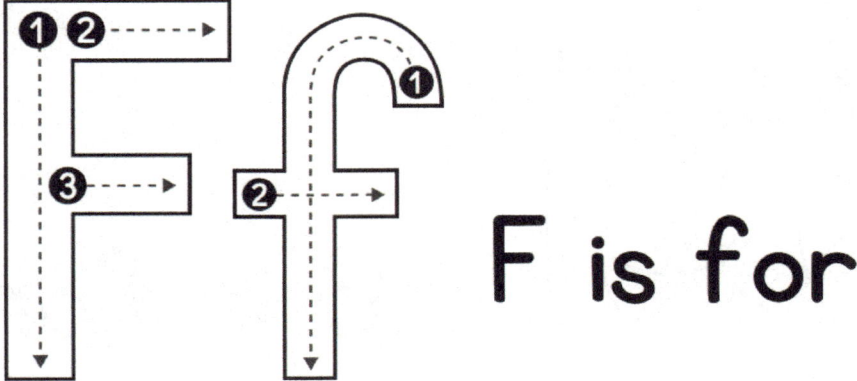

F is for

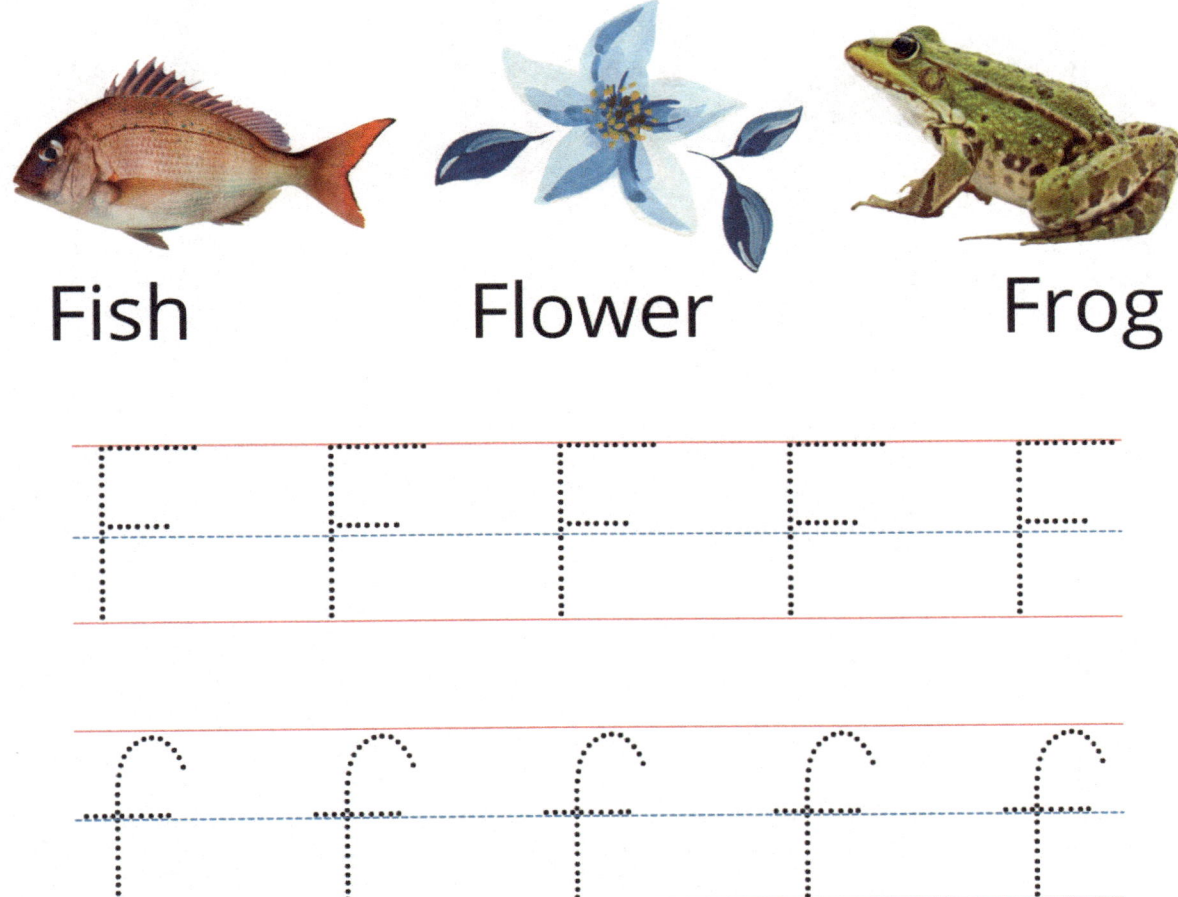

Fish　　　　Flower　　　　Frog

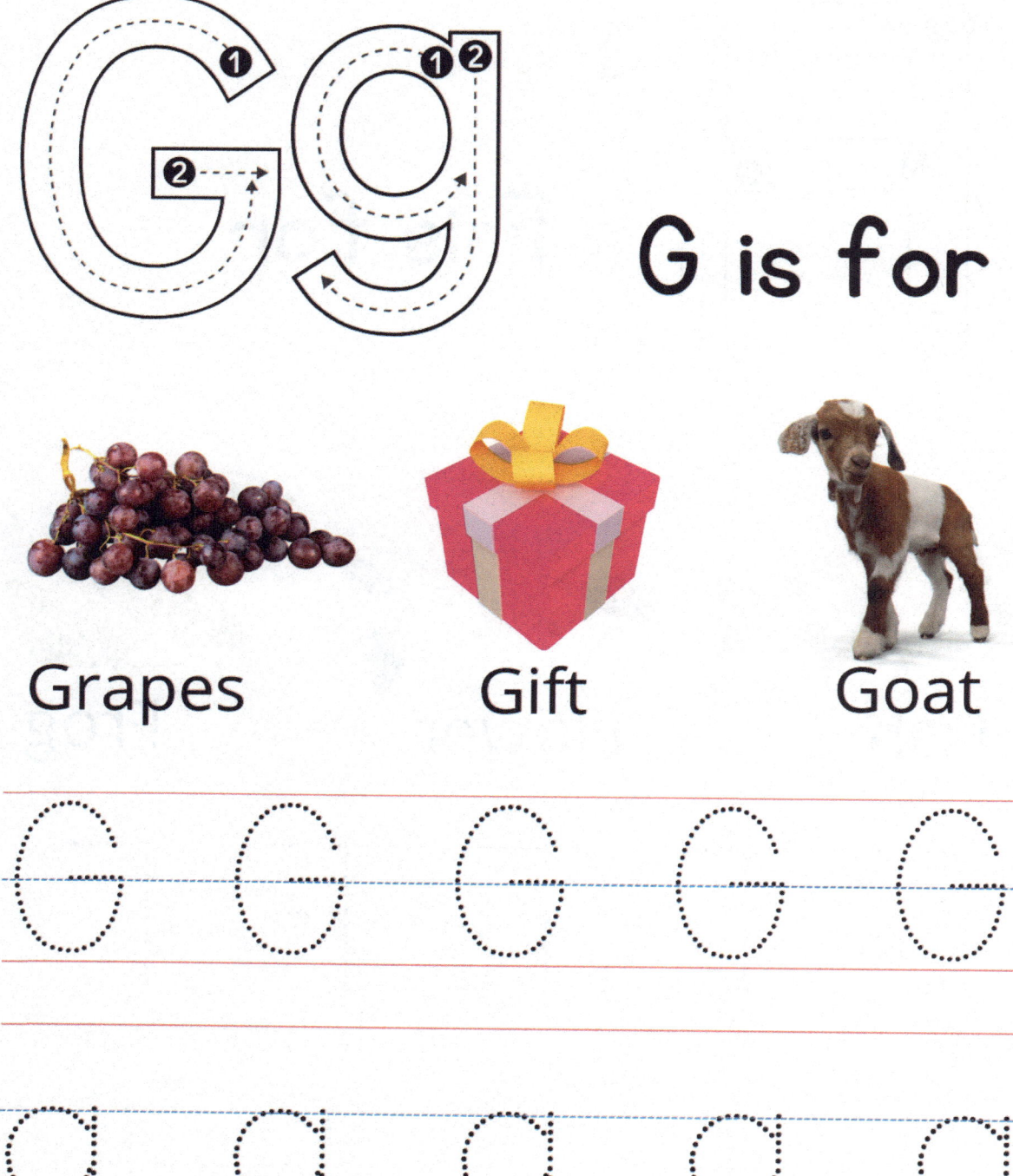

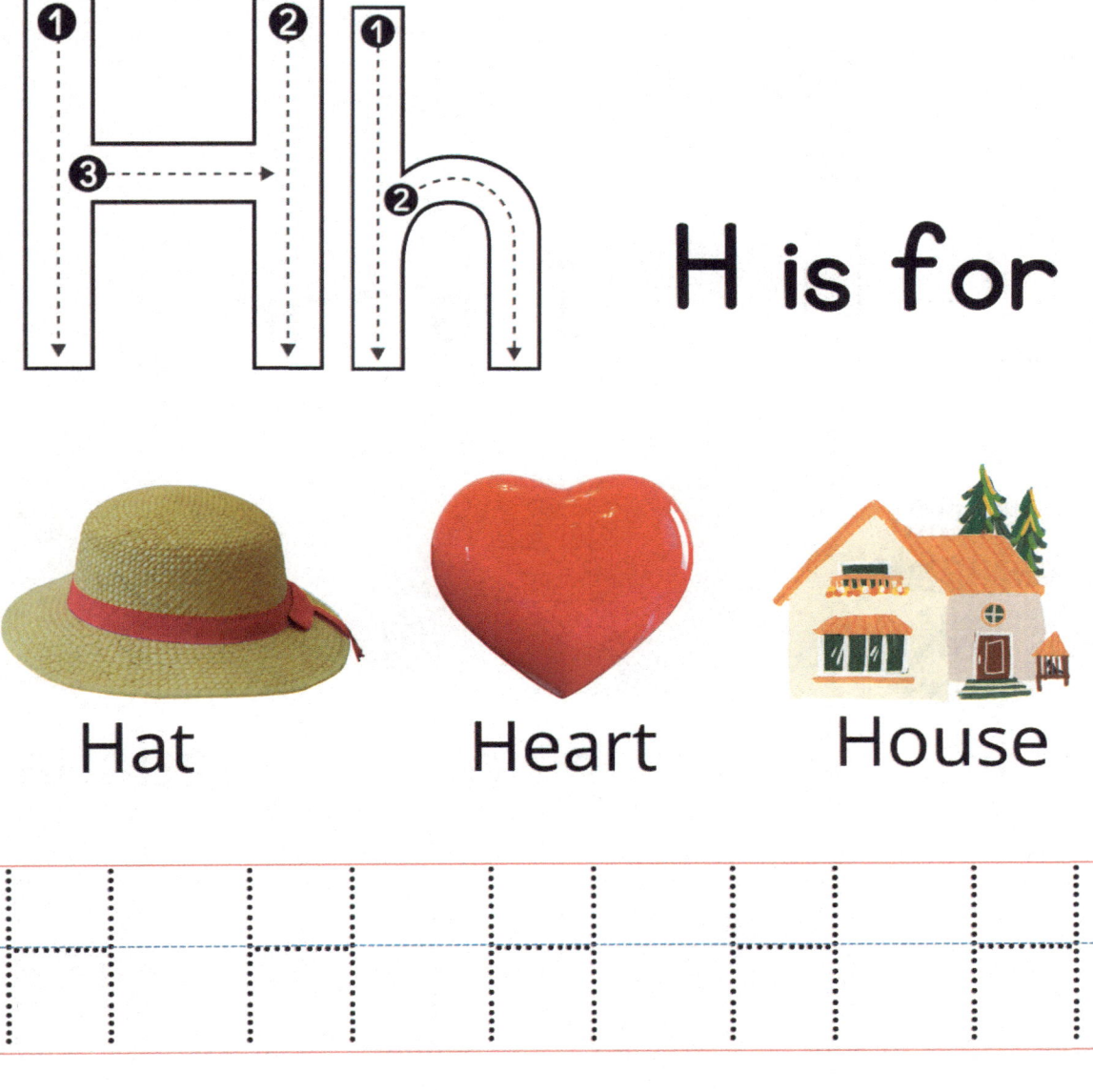

H is for

Hat Heart House

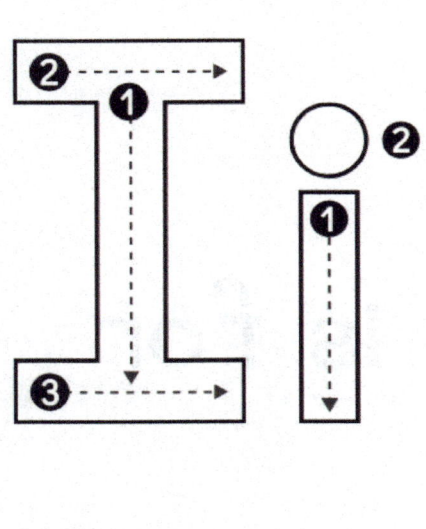

I is for

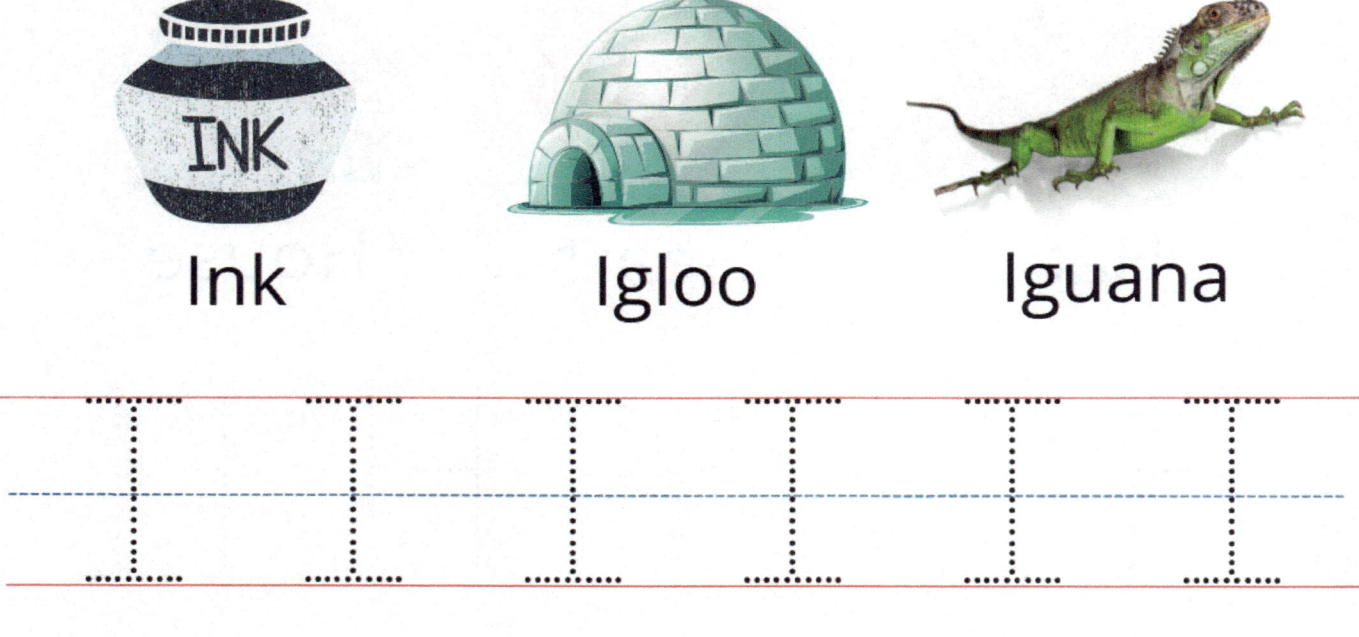

Ink   Igloo   Iguana

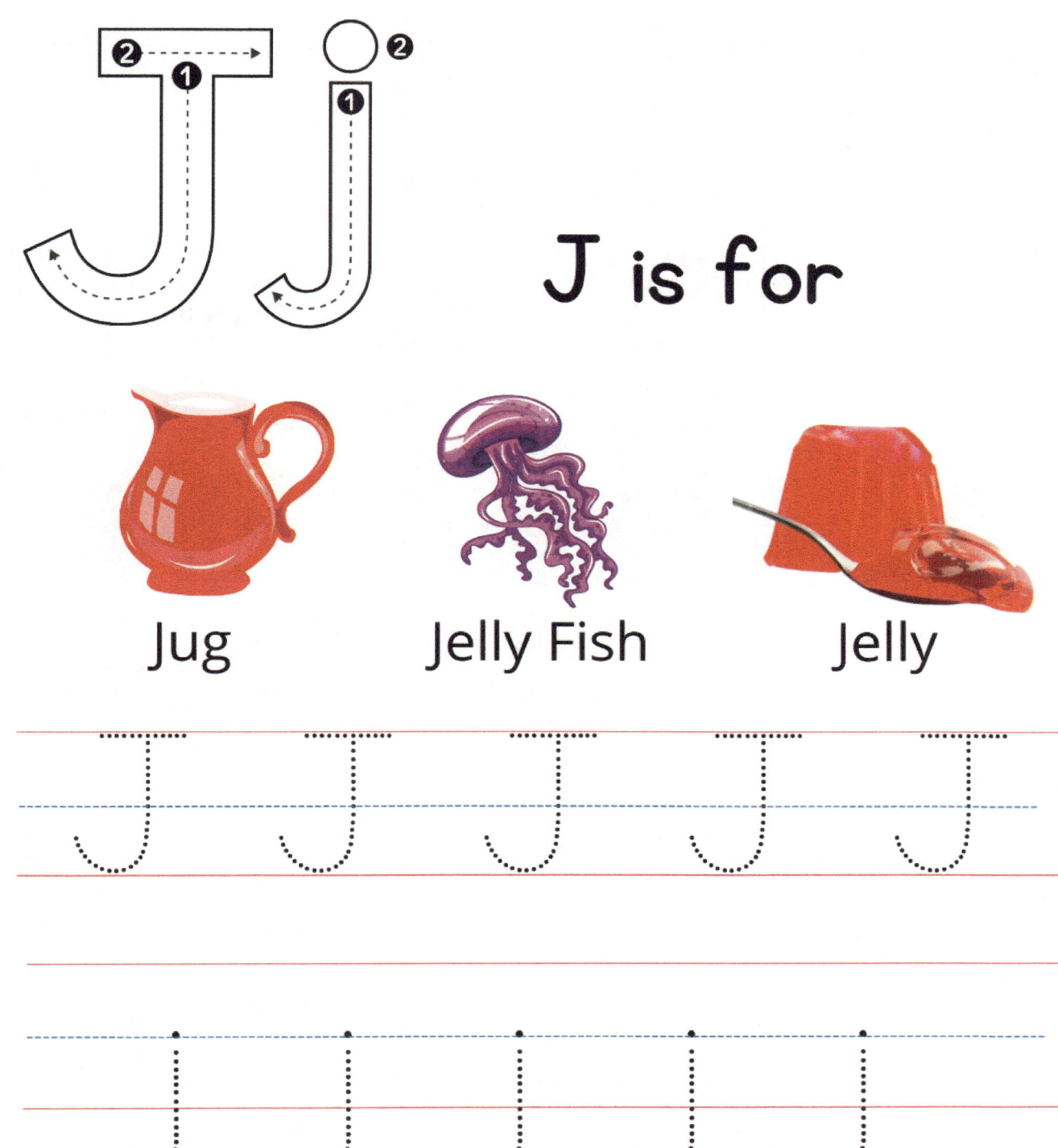

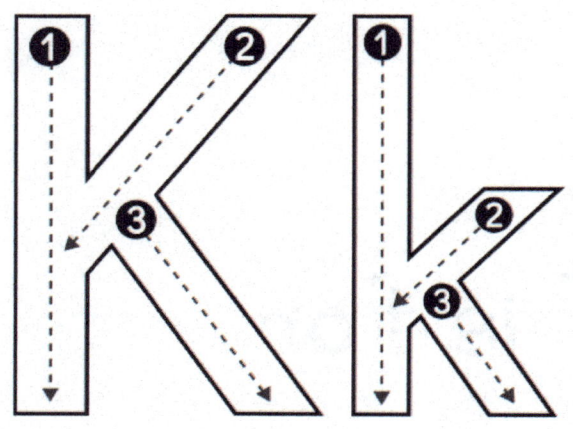

K is for

Kite    Keys    Kangaroo

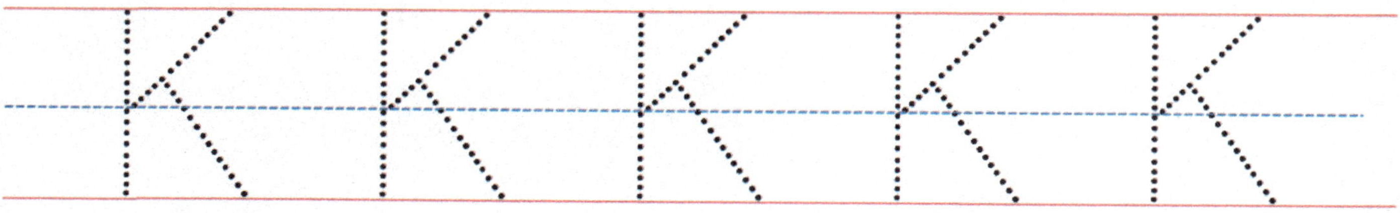

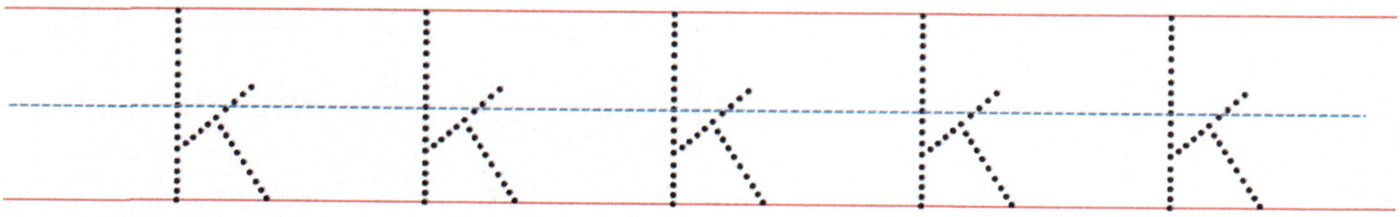

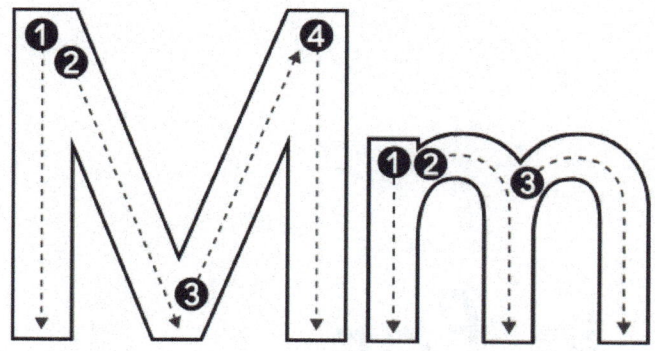

M is for

Mango　　　Mushroom　　　Monkey

M M M M M M

m m m m m m m

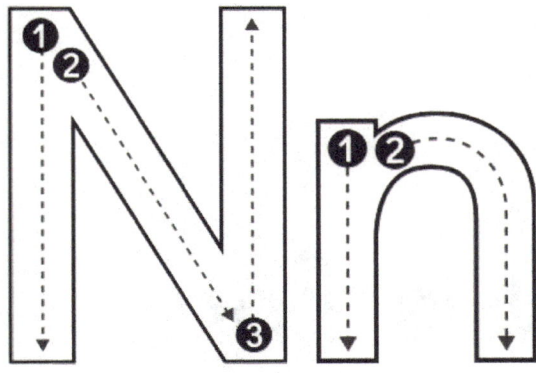

N is for

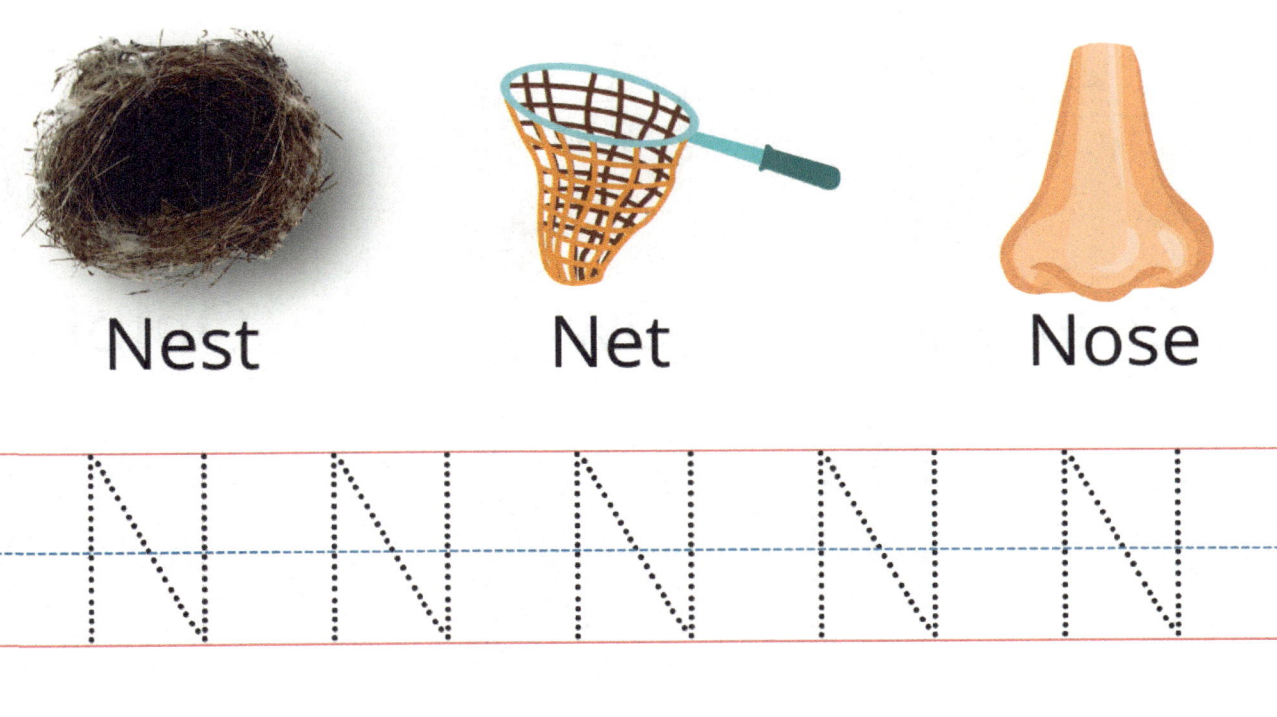

Nest   Net   Nose

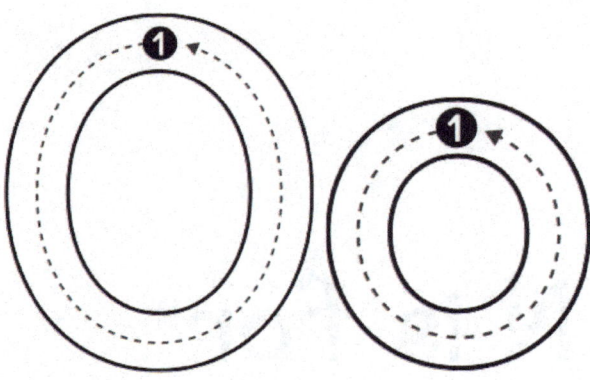 O is for

Orange   Owl   Onion

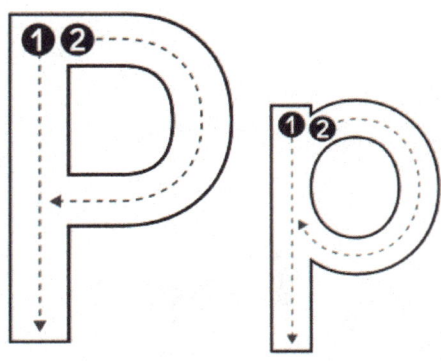

P is for

Parrot

Pineapple

Penguin

P P P P P

p p p p p

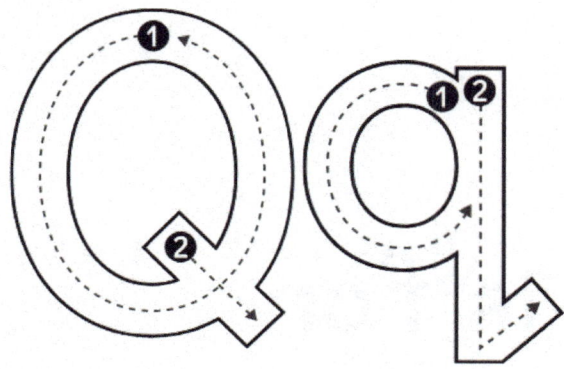

Q is for

Question

Queen

Quail

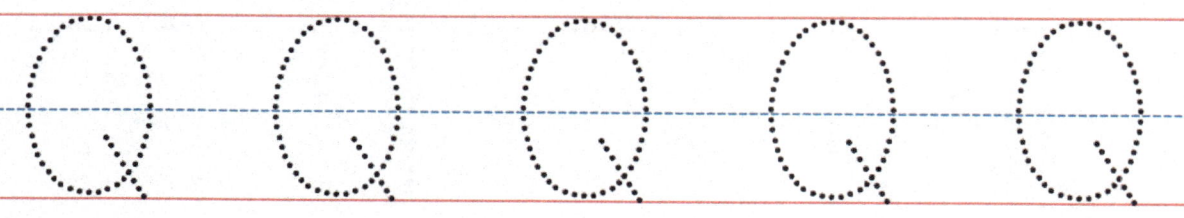

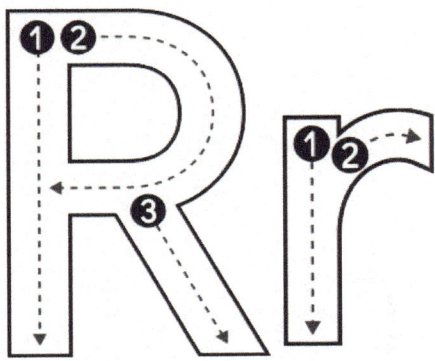

R is for

Rainbow

Rabbit

Rose

S is for

Sun

Spider

Six

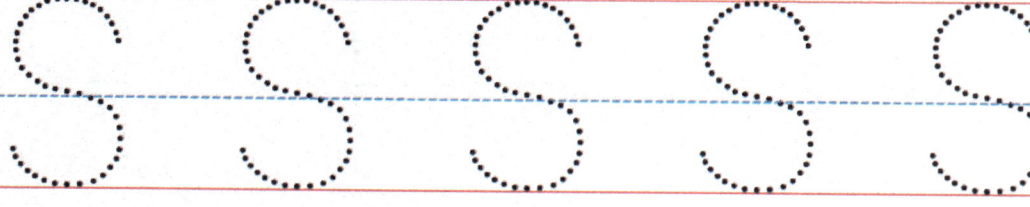

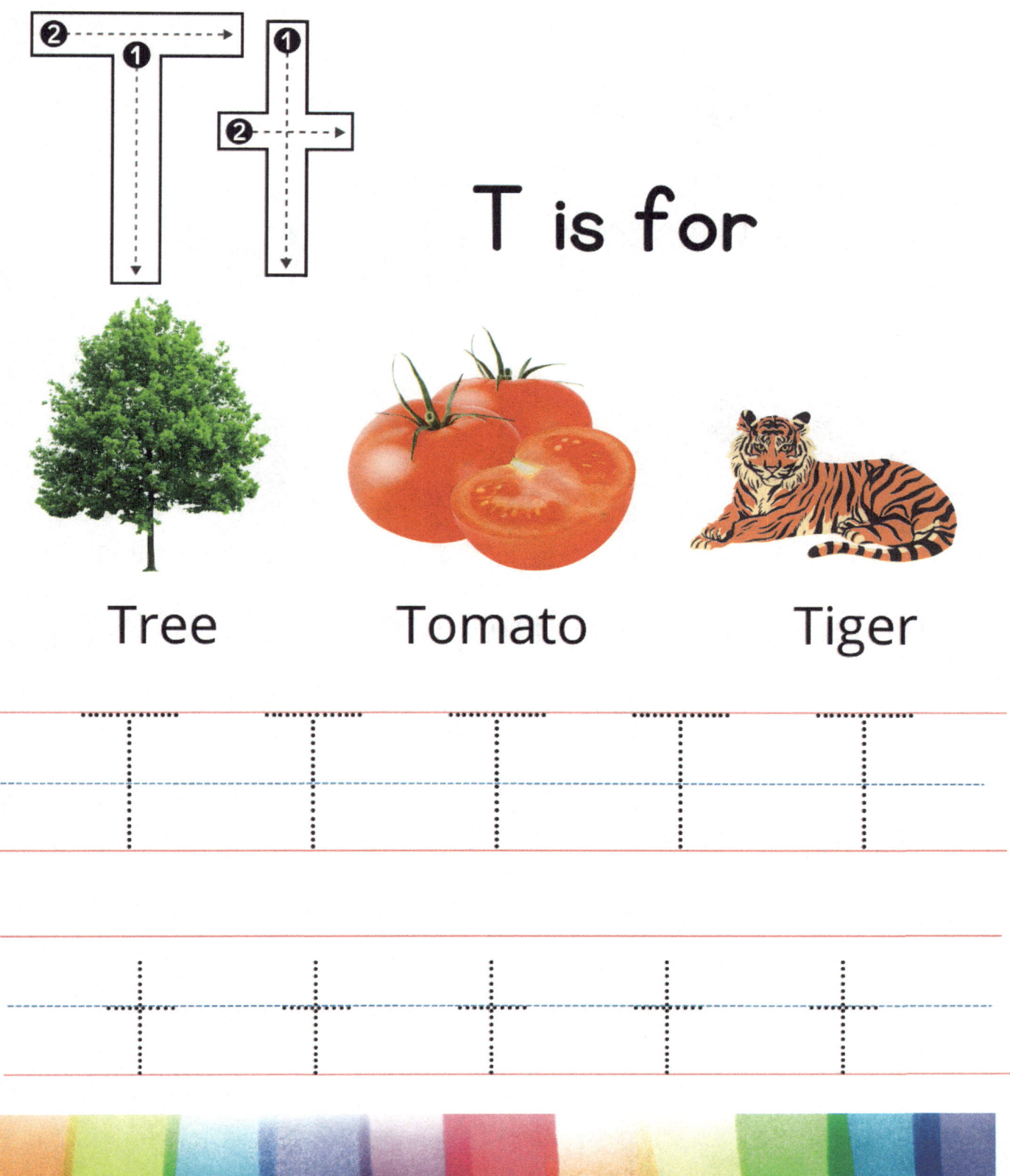

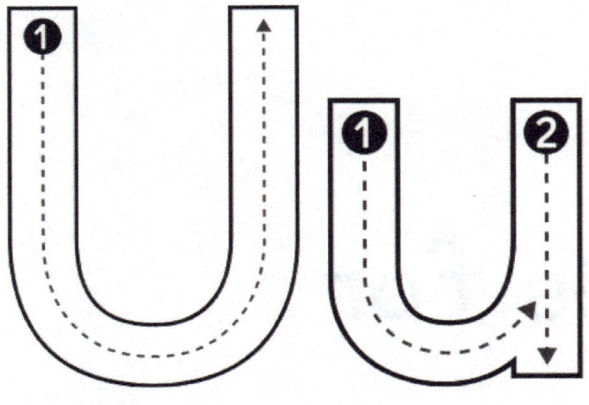 U is for

Umbrella

Unicycle

Uniform

Vv

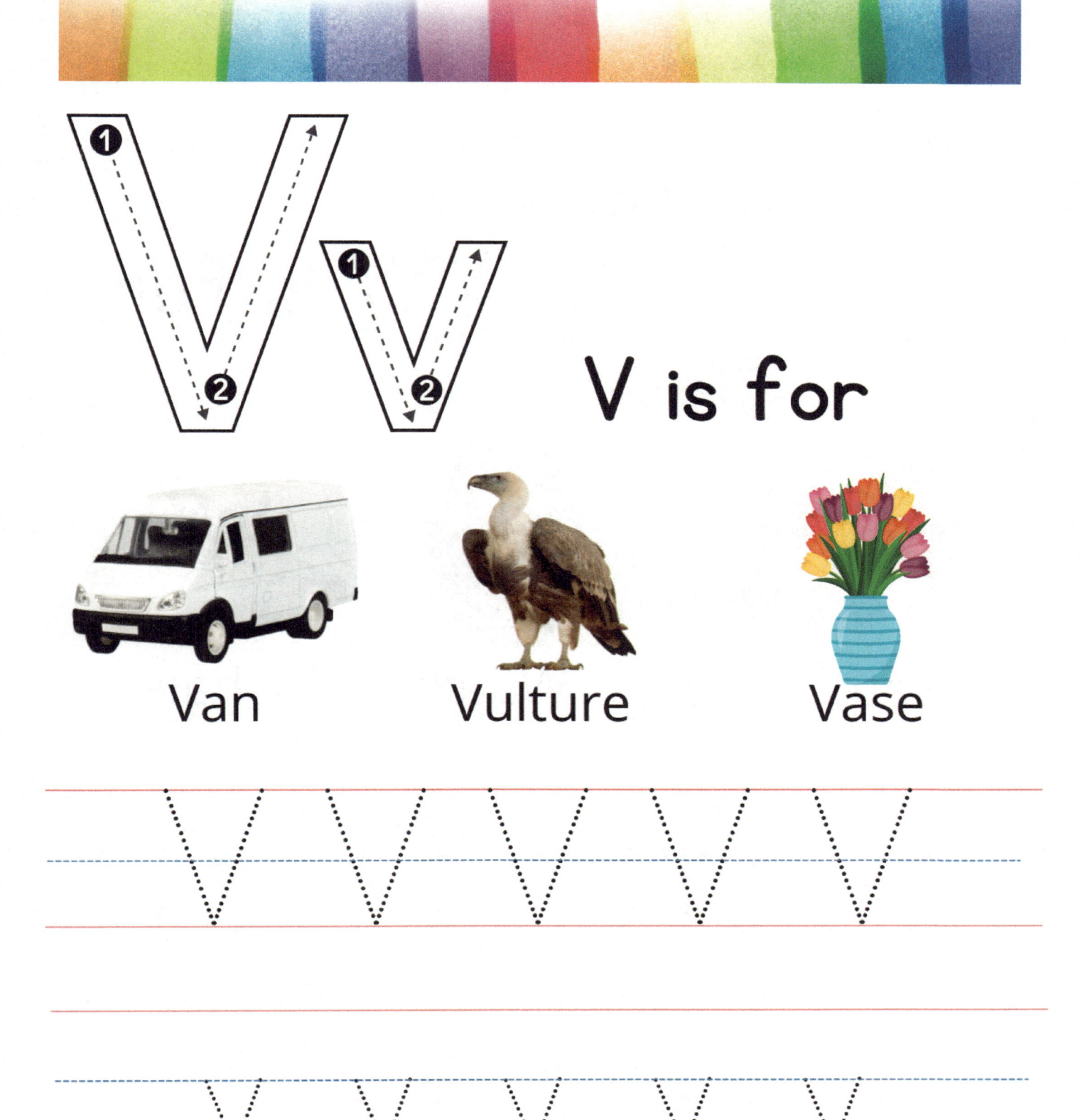

V is for

Van   Vulture   Vase

W w W is for

Watermelon   Watch   Whale

X x

X is for

Xylophone **X- ray** **X- ray Fish**

Y y   Y is for

Yoyo   Yawn   Yacht

Z z

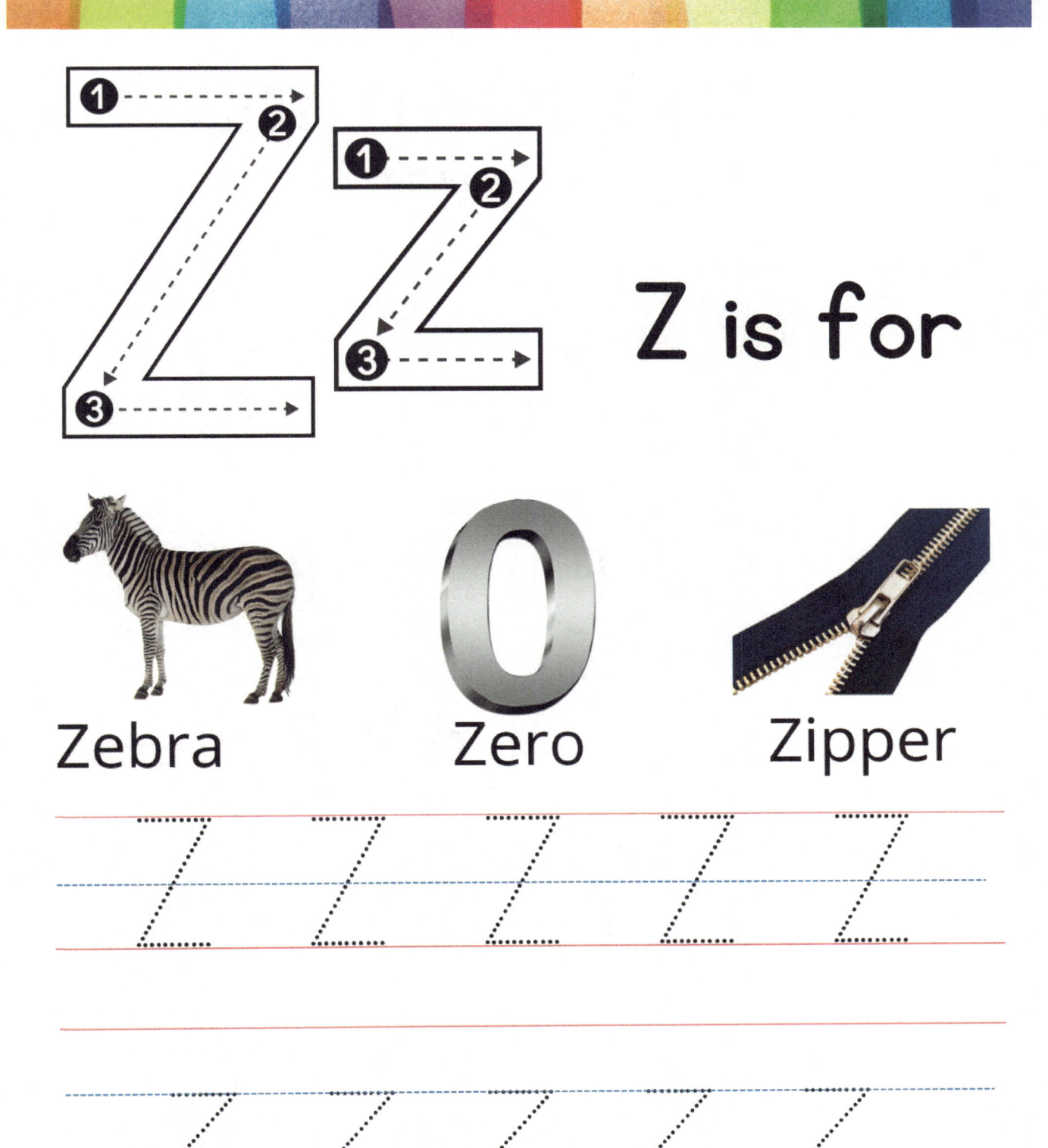

Z is for

Zebra   **Zero**   **Zipper**

FILL THE MISSING LETTERS

Help Mr. Tiger fill in the missing letters on his circle.

A _ C

_ E F _ H I

J _ _ M N _

_ Q R S _ U

V W _ Y Z

Ending Sound of Words

Say the name of each picture and listen to the ending sound. Write the letter that represents that sound then write the word again below each picture.

nu_

pa_

he_

ja_

ma_

bu_

Things we see in school

Trace the words then write them in the space next to it.

Books _____

Bag _____

Pencil _____

Crayons _____

Glue _____

Eraser _____

Picture Matching

Draw a line to match pictures that are related.

MATCHING ANIMALS

Draw a line to match pictures that are the same

Months of the Year

Cut along the dotted lines. Glue the months of the year in the correct order into your scrapbook.

March

June

April

December

September

November

January

October

July

February

May

August

This page intentionally blank

Vehicle Pattern

Cut and paste the correct picture to continue the pattern.

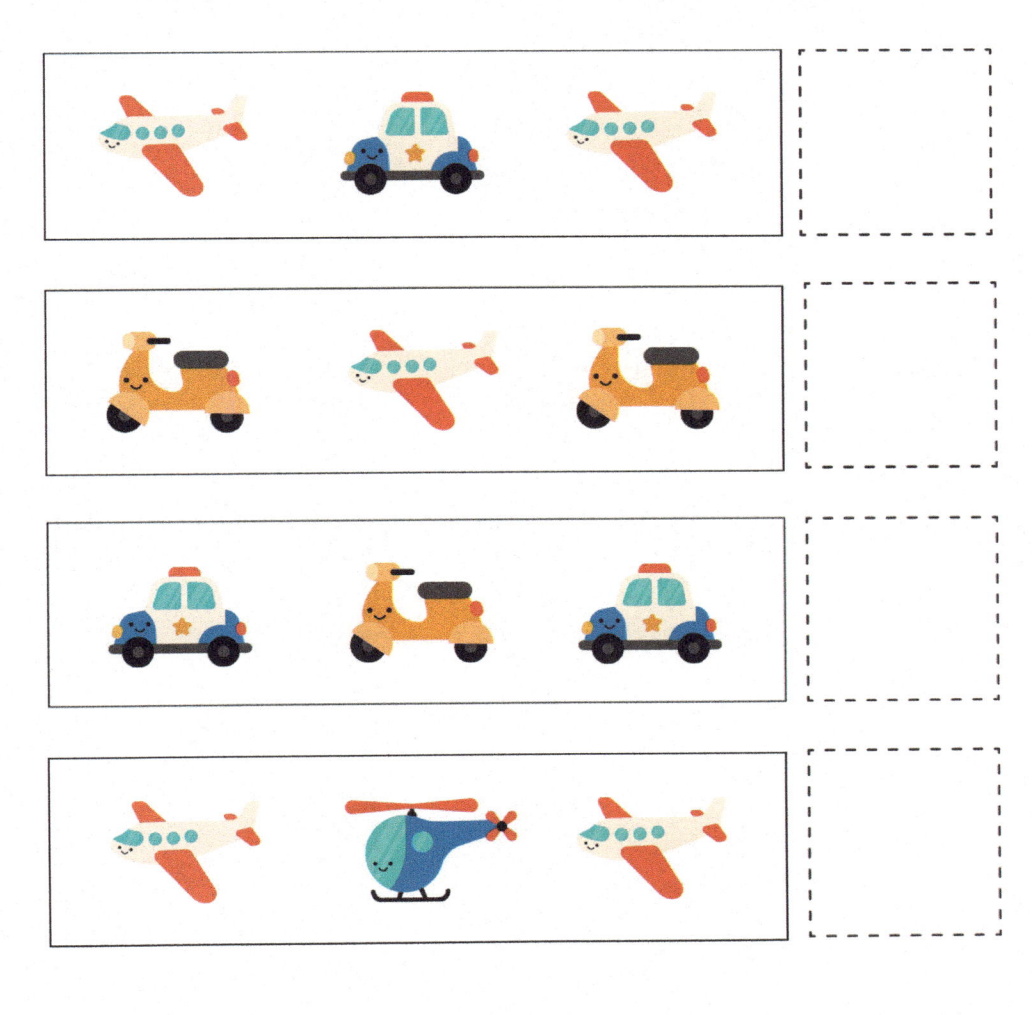

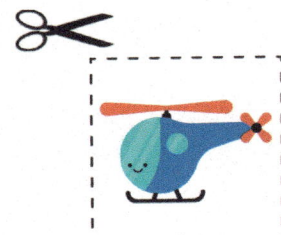

This page intentionally blank

Types of Weather

Look at each weather and Trace the weather name.

Sunny

Rainy

Windy

Stormy

Snowy

Cloudy

Tall or Short?

Tick the tall one.

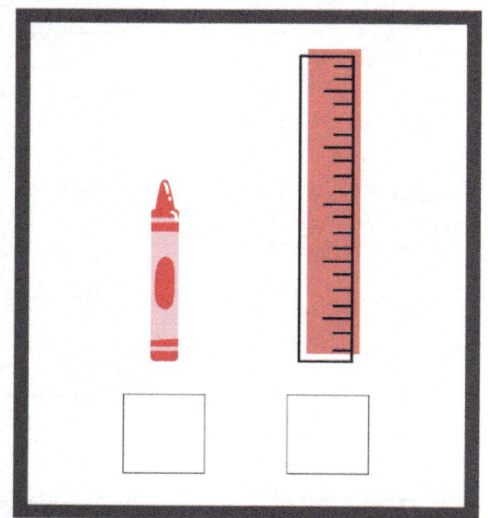

Tick the short one.

WHICH HAS MORE FOOD?

Count the Foods in each box. Put a checkmark on the circle which has more Foods.

MORE OR LESS?

Count the number of fruit then write the correct number on the circle. Compare the two numbers on the circle then choose more or less to complete the sentences.

( ) is (more / less) than ( )

( ) is (more / less) than ( )

( ) is (more / less) than ( )

( ) is (more / less) than ( )

( ) is (more / less) than ( )

Shape Sorters

Cut the pictures, sort and paste them inside the correct box.

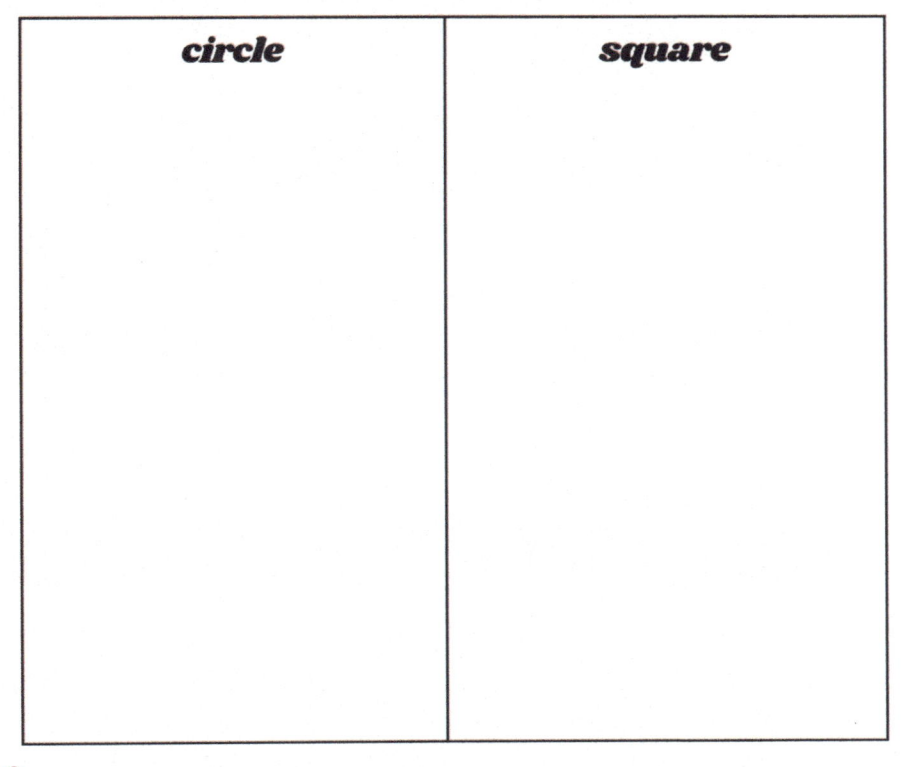

circle	square

This page intentionally blank

UP IN THE SKY

DIRECTIONS: COLOR THE ANIMALS THAT CAN FLY. USE YOUR YELLOW CRAYON.

Back to School Labyrinth

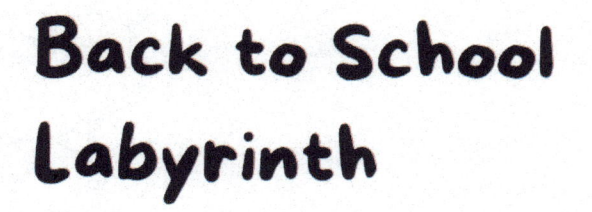

Help the little girl to grab her backpack.

Read and Match

Cut and paste the picture to match each word family –at.

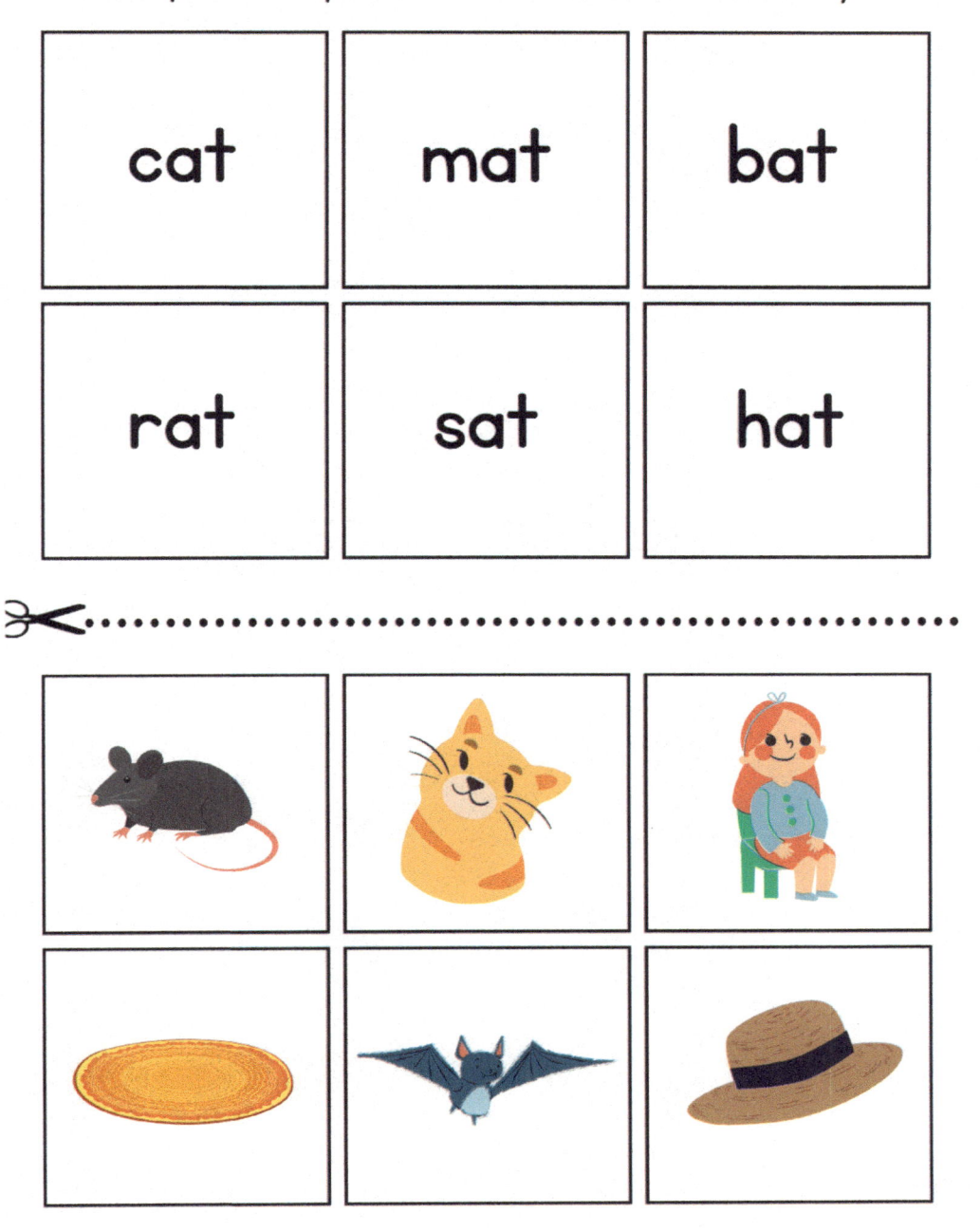

| cat | mat | bat |
| rat | sat | hat |

✂··

This page intentionally blank

I Can Draw Hearts

Help Owliver the Lovely Owl to trace the hearts.

Animal & Food

Read the Name of these Animals and Foods, then draw lines and connects pictures below with the right category.

Peanuts   Elephant   Lion   Apple Jam   Hotdog

Animal   Food

Snail   Pepper   Hippopotamus   Lollipop   X-Ray Fish

Cutting Shapes

Cut out each circle

This page intentionally blank

Cutting Shapes

Let's Complete The Pizza!

This page intentionally blank

Pig mask

Trace the shapes and color your mask

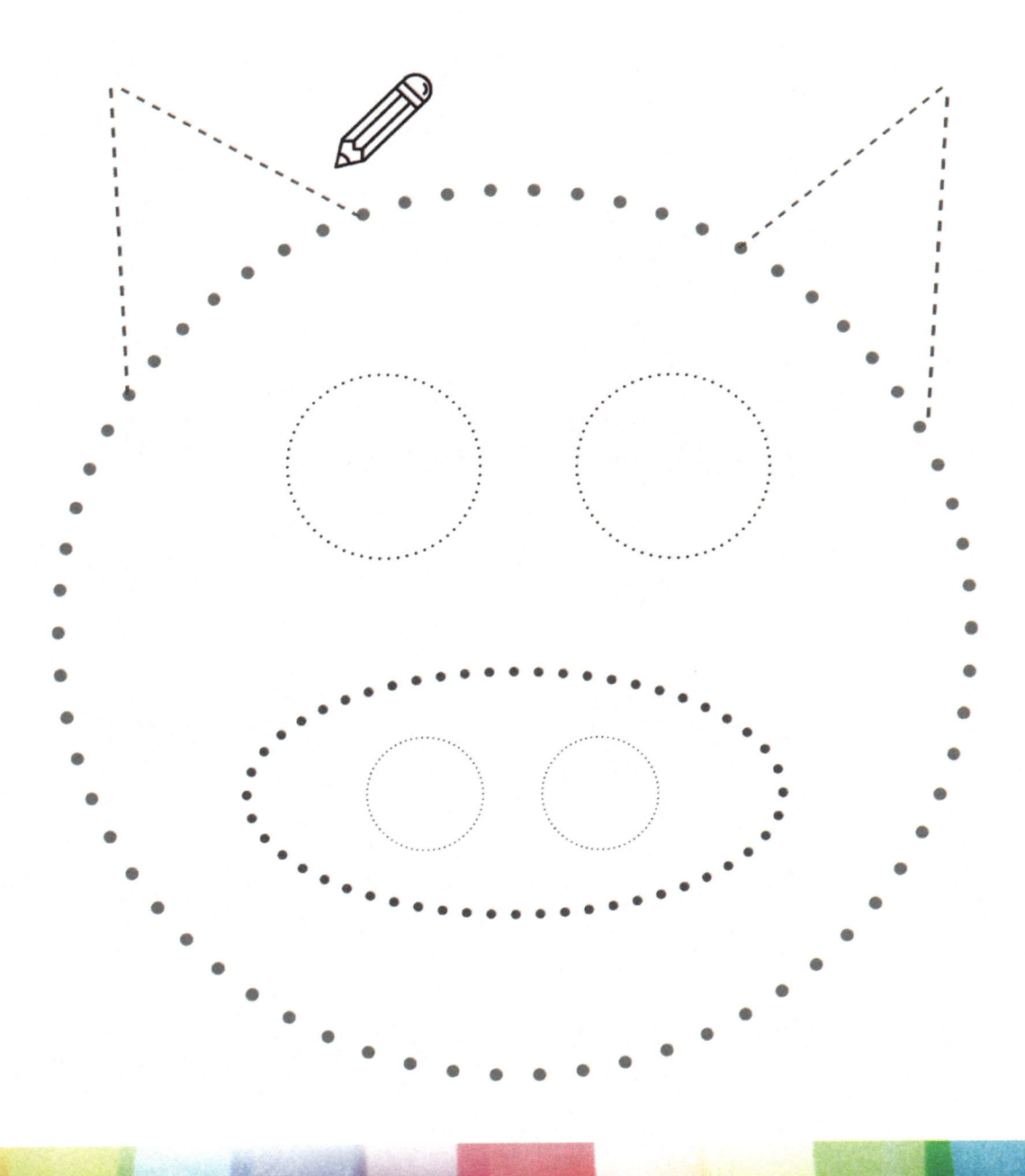

This page intentionally blank

CONNECT THE FARM ANIMALS

Trace the line to connect the farm animals.

Vegetables Shadow Matching

Draw a line from each vegetables to its matching shadow.

Trace the numbers and color the pictures

1
one

Trace the numbers and color the pictures

2
two

2 2 2 2 2
2 2 2 2 2

two two two
two two two

Trace the numbers and color the pictures

3

three

3 3 3 3 3
3 3 3 3 3

three three three
three three three

Trace the numbers and color the pictures

4

four

4 4 4 4 4

4 4 4 4 4

four four four

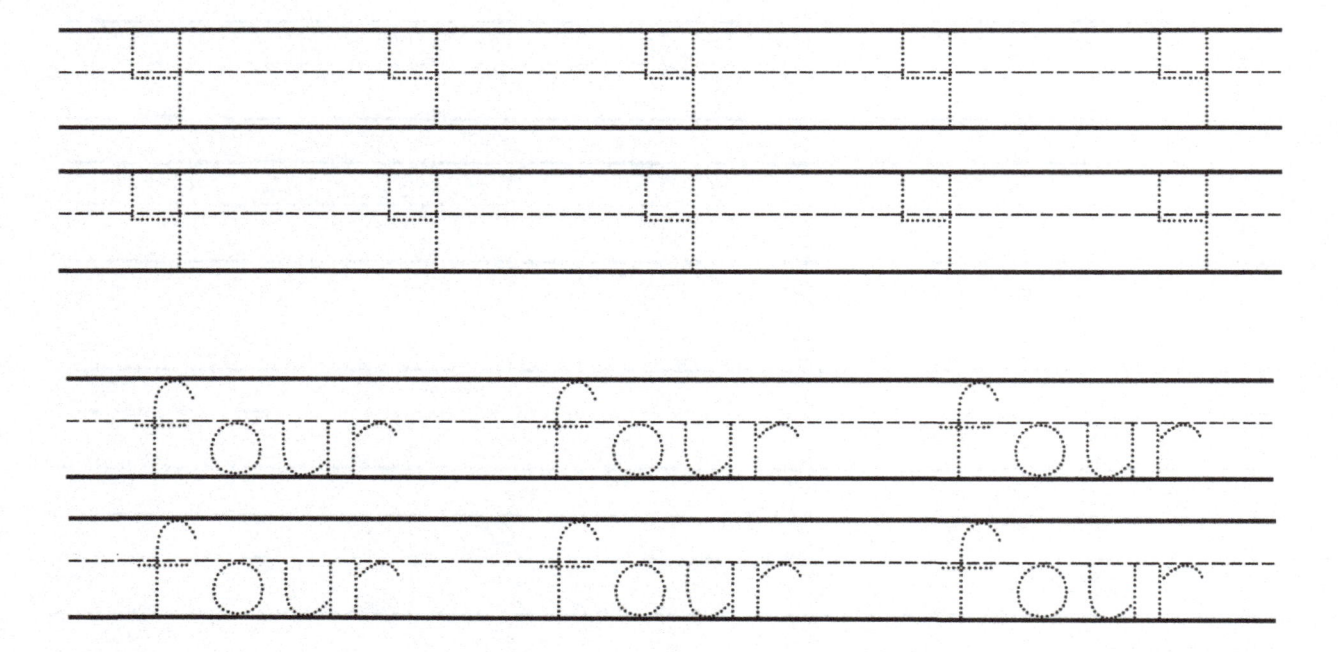

four four four

Trace the numbers and color the pictures

5

five

Trace the numbers and color the pictures

6

six

6 6 6 6 6

6 6 6 6 6

six   six   six

six   six   six

Trace the numbers and color the pictures

7
seven

Trace the numbers and color the pictures

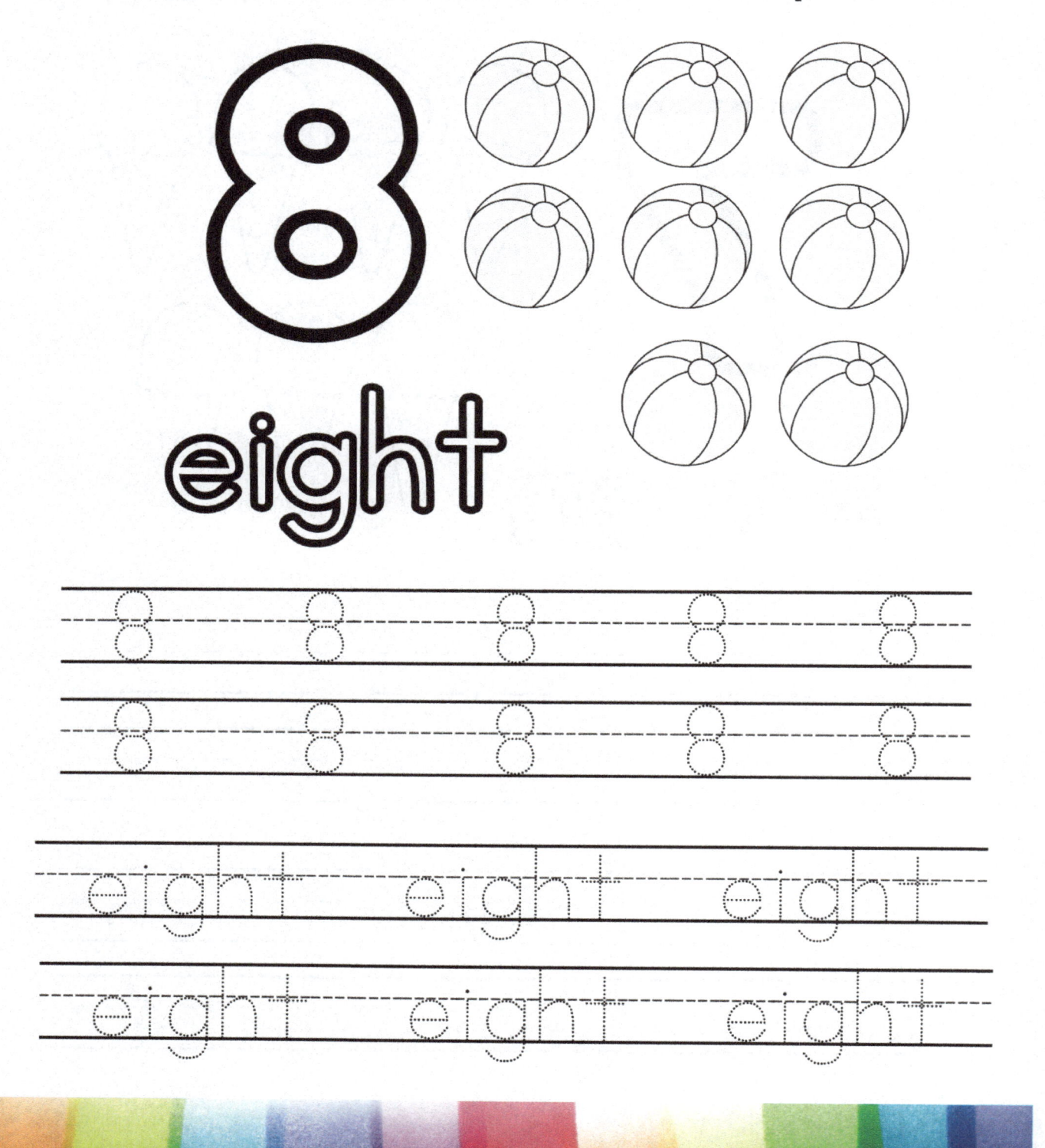

8
eight

Trace the numbers and color the pictures

9

nine

9 9 9 9 9

9 9 9 9 9

nine nine nine

nine nine nine

Trace the numbers and color the pictures

10

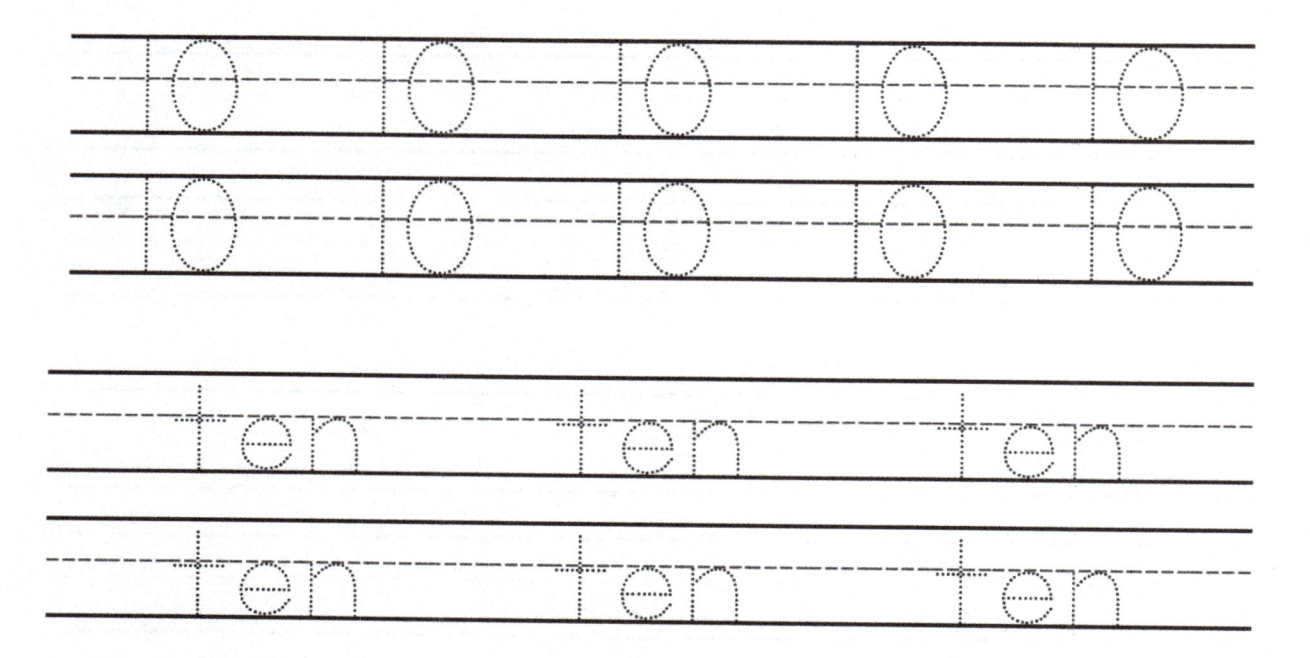

ten

Trace the numbers and color the pictures

11
eleven

eleven eleven
eleven eleven

Trace the numbers and color the pictures

12
twelve

12 12 12 12 12

12 12 12 12 12

twelve twelve

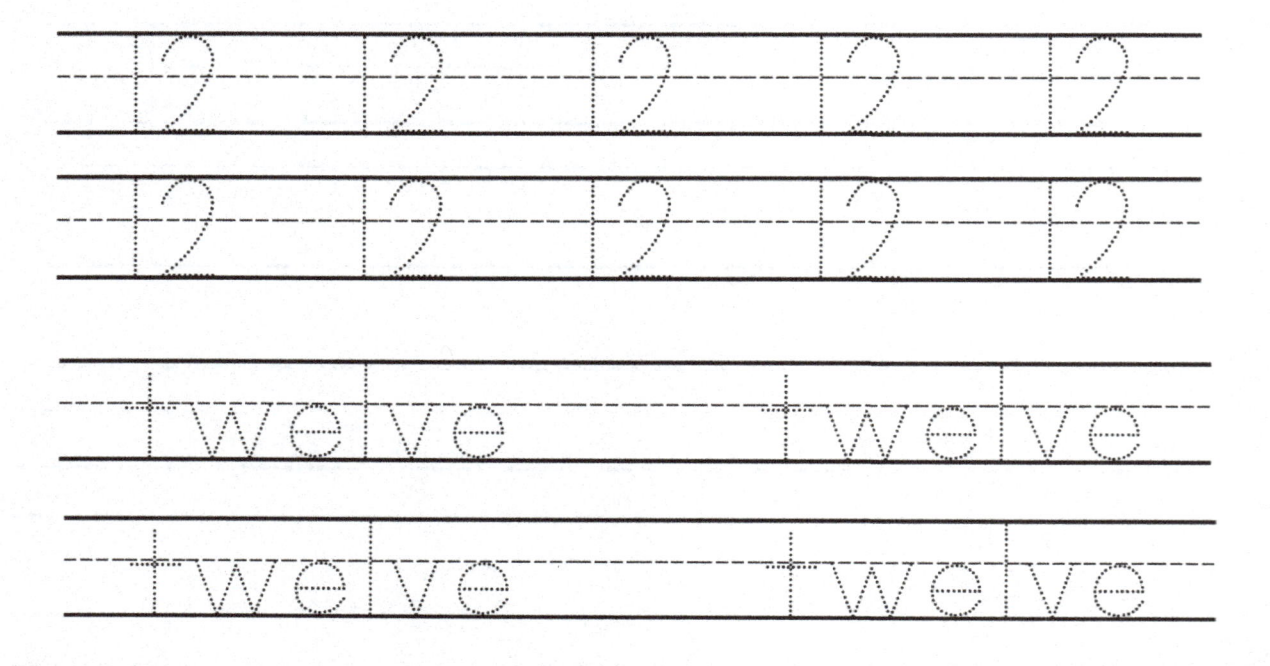

twelve twelve

Trace the numbers and color the pictures

13

thirteen

13 13 13 13 13

13 13 13 13 13

thirteen thirteen

thirteen thirteen

Trace the numbers and color the pictures

14

fourteen

Trace the numbers and color the pictures

15
fifteen

15 15 15 15 15

15 15 15 15 15

fifteen fifteen

fifteen fifteen

Trace the numbers and color the pictures

16
sixteen

16 16 16 16 16
16 16 16 16 16

sixteen sixteen
sixteen sixteen

Trace the numbers and color the pictures

17

seventeen

17 17 17 17 17
17 17 17 17 17

seventeen seventeen
seventeen seventeen

Trace the numbers and color the pictures

18

eighteen

18 18 18 18 18
18 18 18 18 18

eighteen   eighteen
eighteen   eighteen

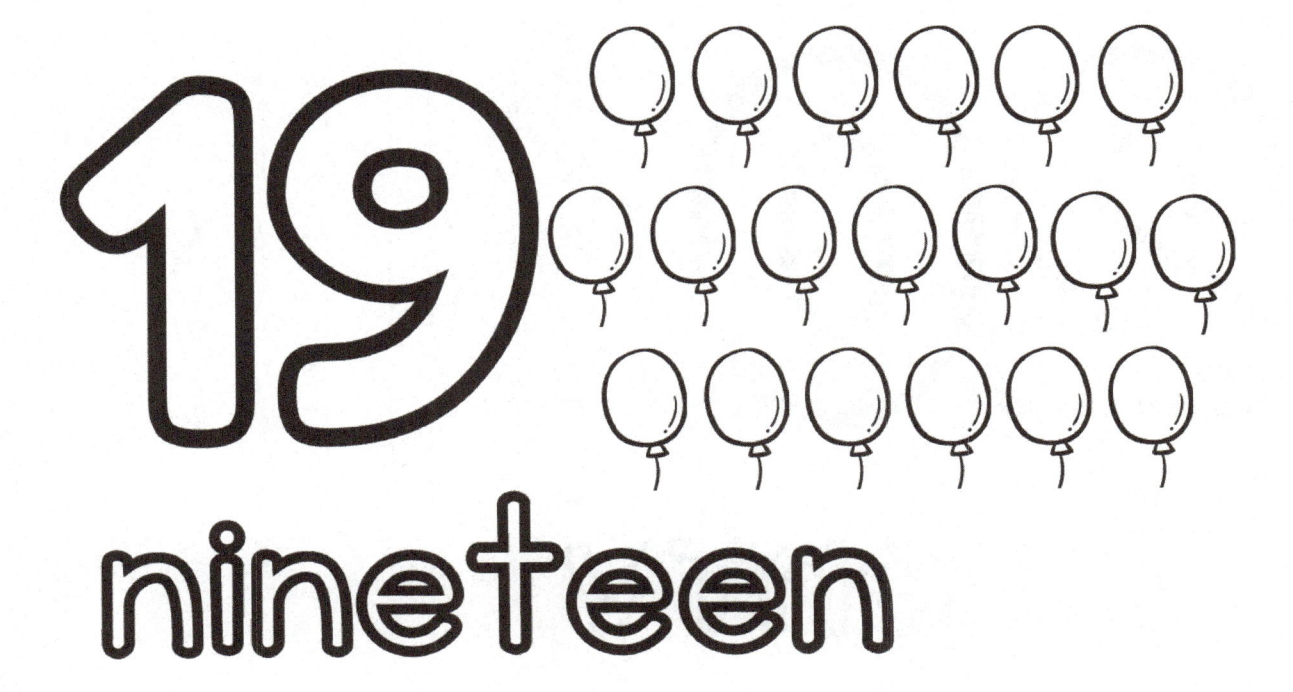

Trace the numbers and color the pictures

19
nineteen

Trace the numbers and color the pictures

20
twenty

20 20 20 20 20
20 20 20 20 20

twenty twenty
twenty twenty

MISSING NUMBERS

Fill the missing numbers to complete the sequence on each row.

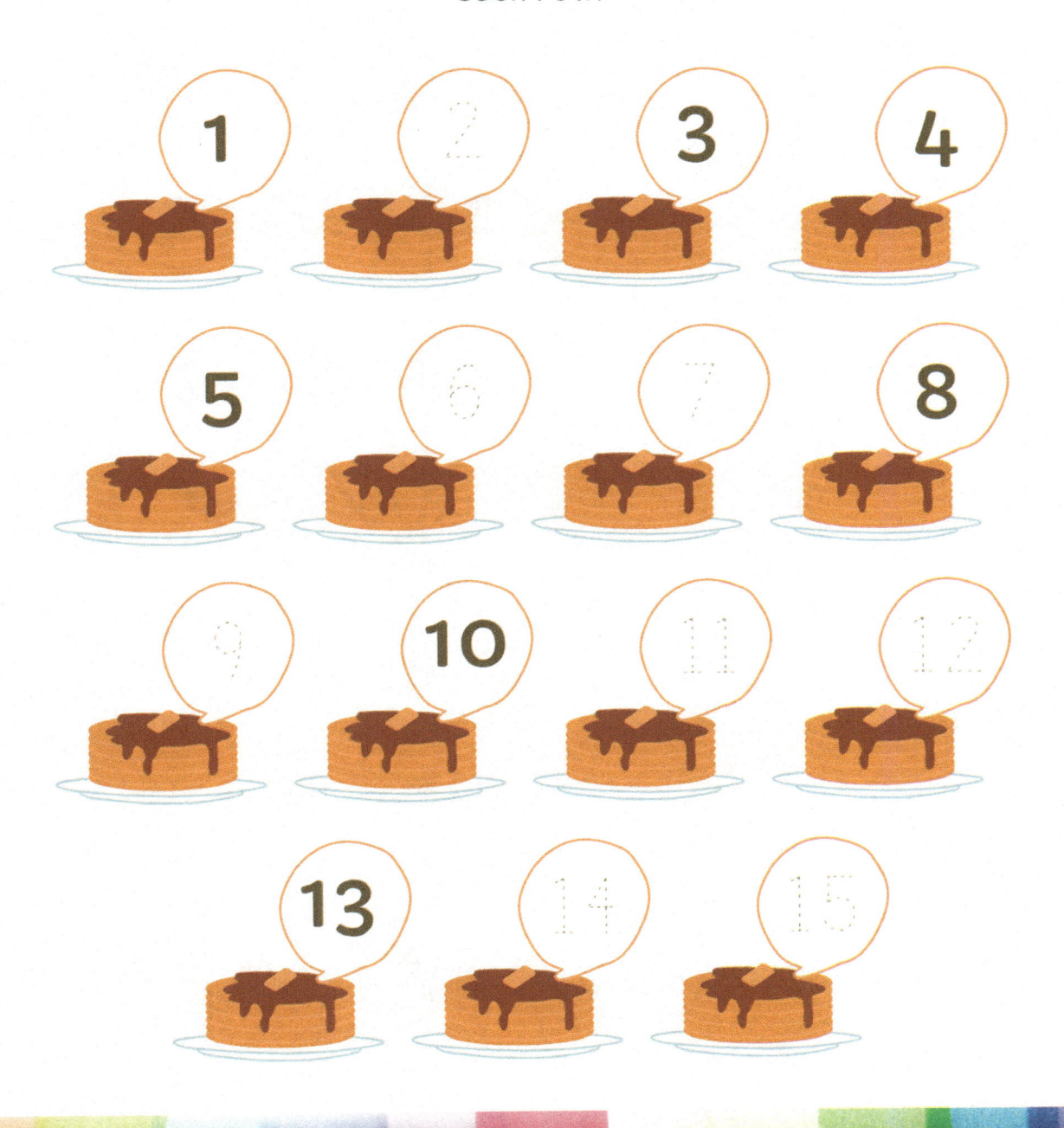

1 2 3 4

5 6 7 8

9 10 11 12

13 14 15

Sunflower Matching

Draw a line to match the number with the correct number of sunflowers

5

2

6

3

8

4

9

COLOR BY NUMBERS

Color Key

| 1 Red | 2 Yellow | 3 Green | 4 Brown |

COUNT & MARK

Count the space elements in each box
and mark the correct number

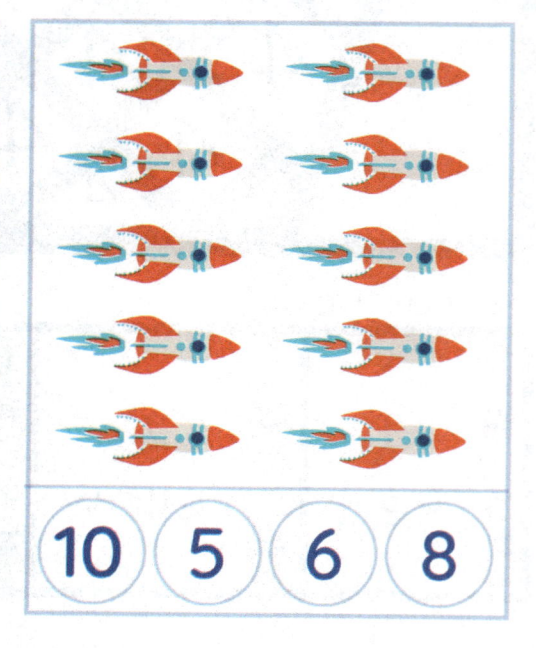

5 9 2 1

1 3 6 5

7 8 9 6

10 5 6 8

COUNTING BUGS

How many bugs do you count?
Color the correct number of dots.

Monster Count!

8 6 5	9 10 12
8 7 11	15 20 25

Parts of a Plant

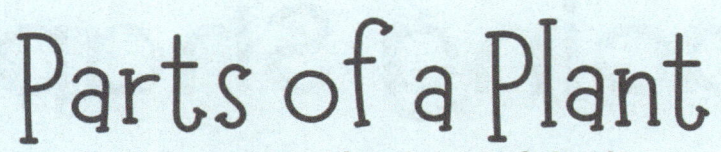

Write in the name of each part of the plant.

leaf   root   fruit   bud   stem   flower

Tracing Shapes

Square

Circle

Hexagon

Rectangle

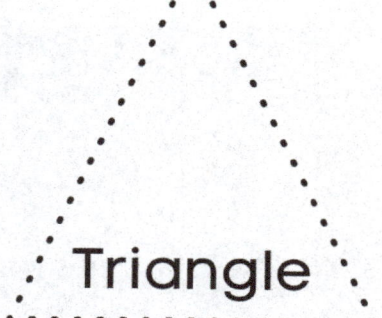

Triangle

Star

KIDS & BALLOONS

Trace the lines and color the balloons. Boys green, girls orange.

NUMBER MATCHING

Circle the correct number to match the number.

Nine — 4   9   11

Eight — 6   8   9

Five — 5   6   15

Ten — 10   15   20

Eleven — 8   10   11

Twenty — 19   20   22

Twelve — 11   12   14

Sixteen — 15   16   19

Seventeen — 16   17   18

Telling Time to the Hour

Which digital clock shows the same time as the analog clock? Circle the correct answer.

Puppy Treats

Help the puppies get to the treats. Trace the lines to show each puppy the treat!

Under the Sea

Count the number of objects and circle the correct answer.

3 5 4 6	7 4 5 3

9 8 10 7	6 2 1 3

Circle Maze

- Deliver the Mother Dragon to her egg.

COUNTING 1-5
CUT AND PASTE ACTIVITY

Instructions: Count the flowers. Match the flowers to its corresponding flower pots.

1 2 3

4 5

This page intentionally blank

BEFORE AND AFTER

Write the numbers that come before and after.

1 __ 3	__ 6 7
4 5 __	2 __ 4
__ 2 3	5 6 __
__ 8 9	6 __ 8
2 __ 4	5 6 __

FIRST, SECOND OR LAST

Circle the first, second or last space element.

FIRST

LAST

SECOND

LAST

LAST

SECOND

COLOR BY NUMBER

1. RED
2. YELLOW
3. PURPLE
4. BLUE
5. GREEN
6. ORANGE

Our School Bag

- What do you have in your school bag? Draw a line.

SYMMETRY

Trace and color to make a symmetrical bear:

CAN YOU DO IT?

Directions: Read the questions and circle your answer.

Can you ride a bicycle?

Yes, I can.   No, I can't.

Can you climb a tree?

Yes, I can.   No, I can't.

Can you swim?

Yes, I can.   No, I can't.

Can you sing a song?

Yes, I can.   No, I can't.

Can you dance?

Yes, I can.   No, I can't.

✂ Days of the Week

Cut along the dotted lines. Glue the days of the week in the correct order into your scrapbook.

Saturday

Monday

Wednesday

Friday

Sunday

Tuesday

Thursday

This page intentionally blank

Color by Number

Use the code to color the picture.

- 2 green
- 3 red
- 4 brown
- 5 yellow
- 6 blue
- 7 black

Ordinal Numbers

Write the ordinal number indicated by the colored fruit.

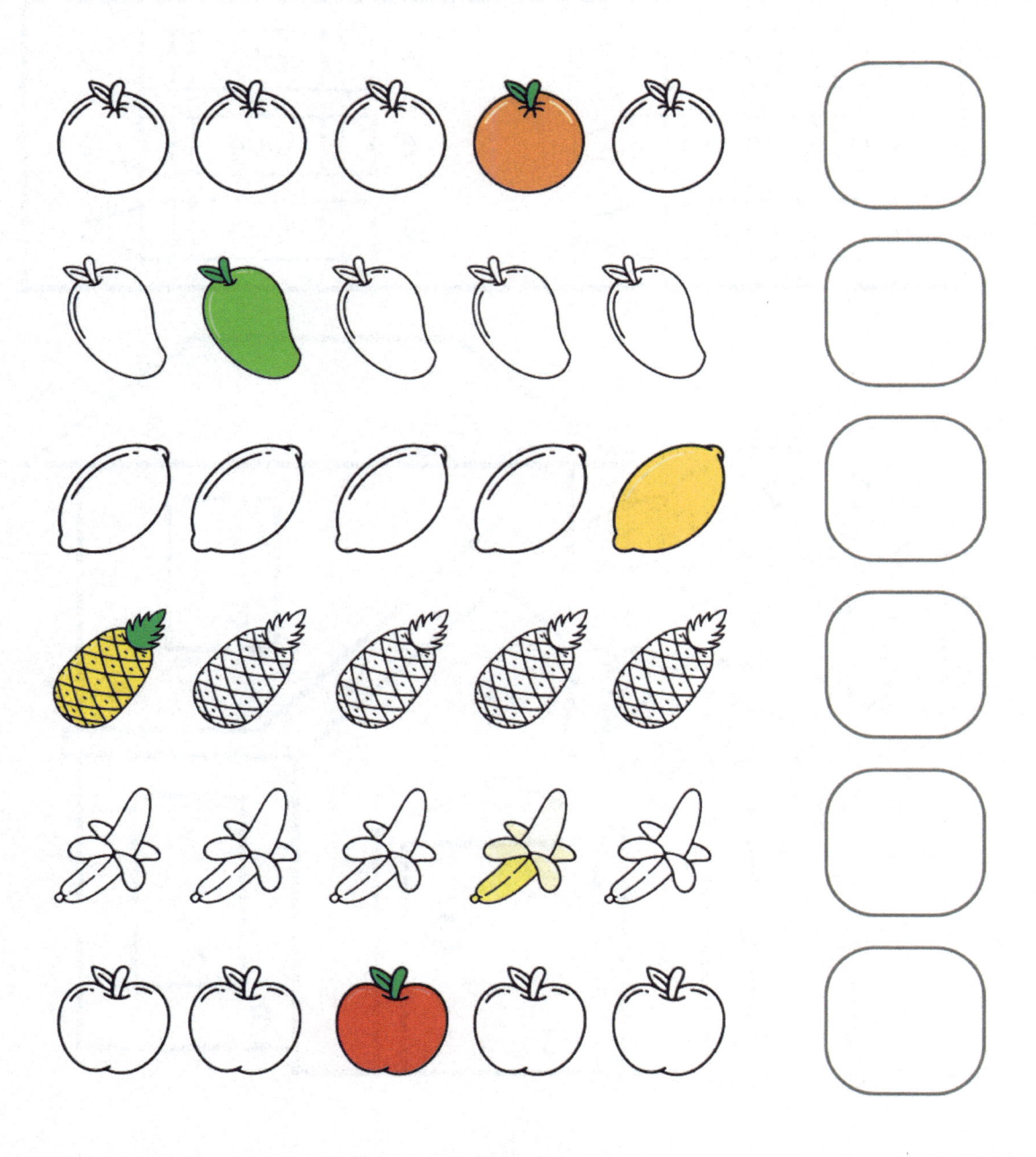

Number Matching

Draw a line matching the numerals and the numbers represented with the hands.

2
1
4
3
5

Trace and Match

Match the correct number of shape to their numerals and trace the number.

1 •

2 •

3 •

4 •

5 •

6 •

Dot-to-Dot

Connect the dots from 1 to 25, this way you practice counting and discover a very tasty piece of fruit.

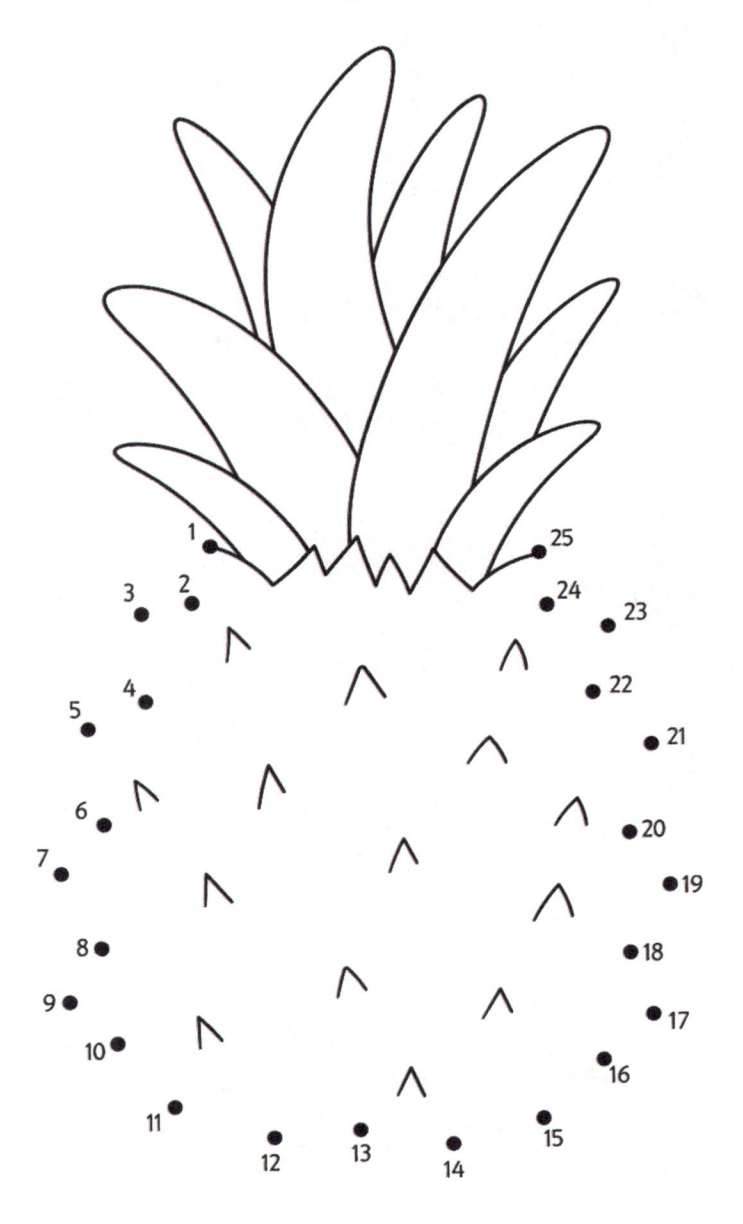

OBJECT ADDITION

Add the images. Draw a line between the total number of images on each box and the number on the right.

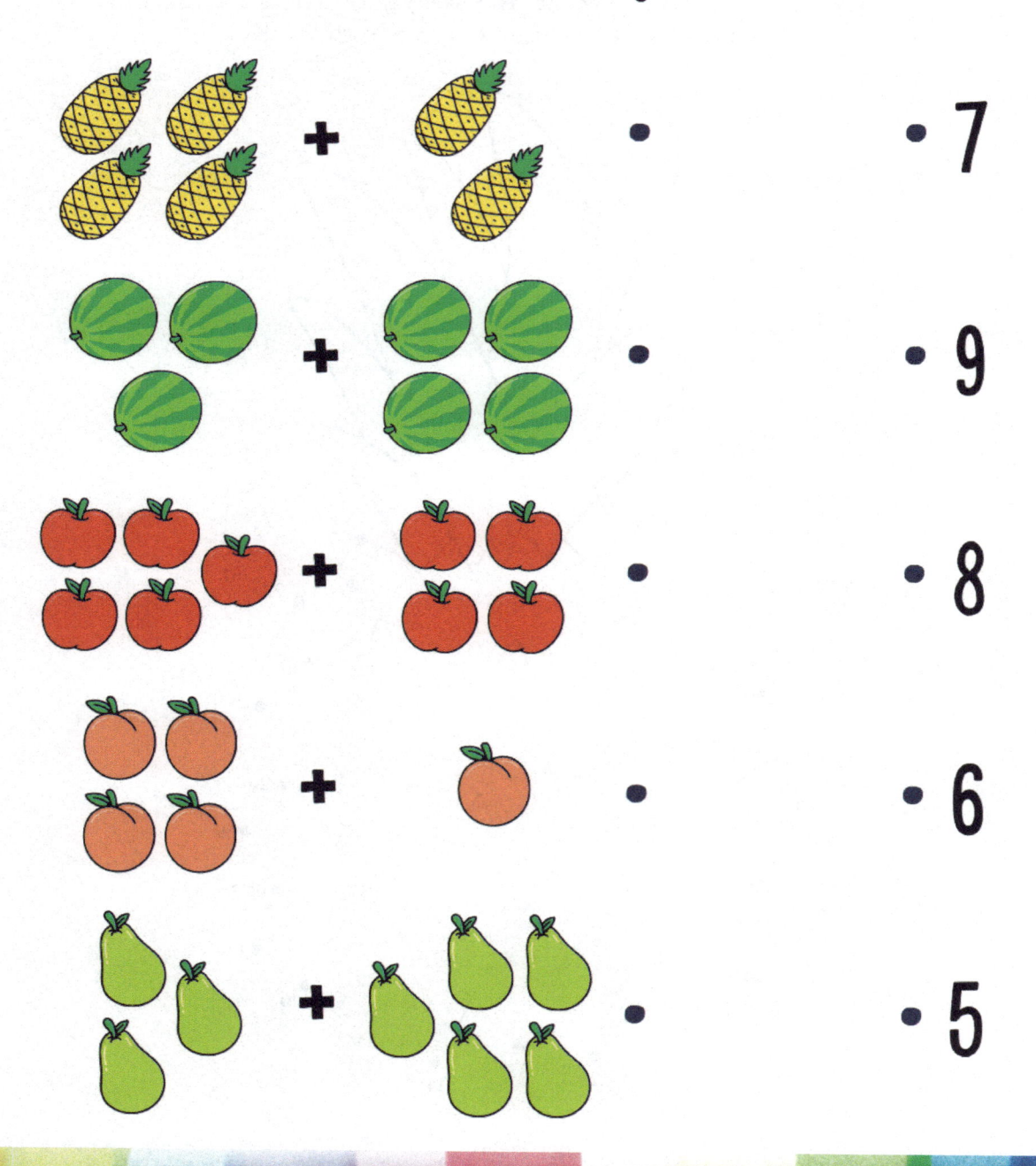

- 4 pineapples + 2 pineapples • • 7
- 3 watermelons + 4 watermelons • • 9
- 5 apples + 3 apples • • 8
- 4 oranges + 1 orange • • 6
- 3 pears + 4 pears • • 5

SYMMETRY

Trace and color to make a symmetrical watermelon:

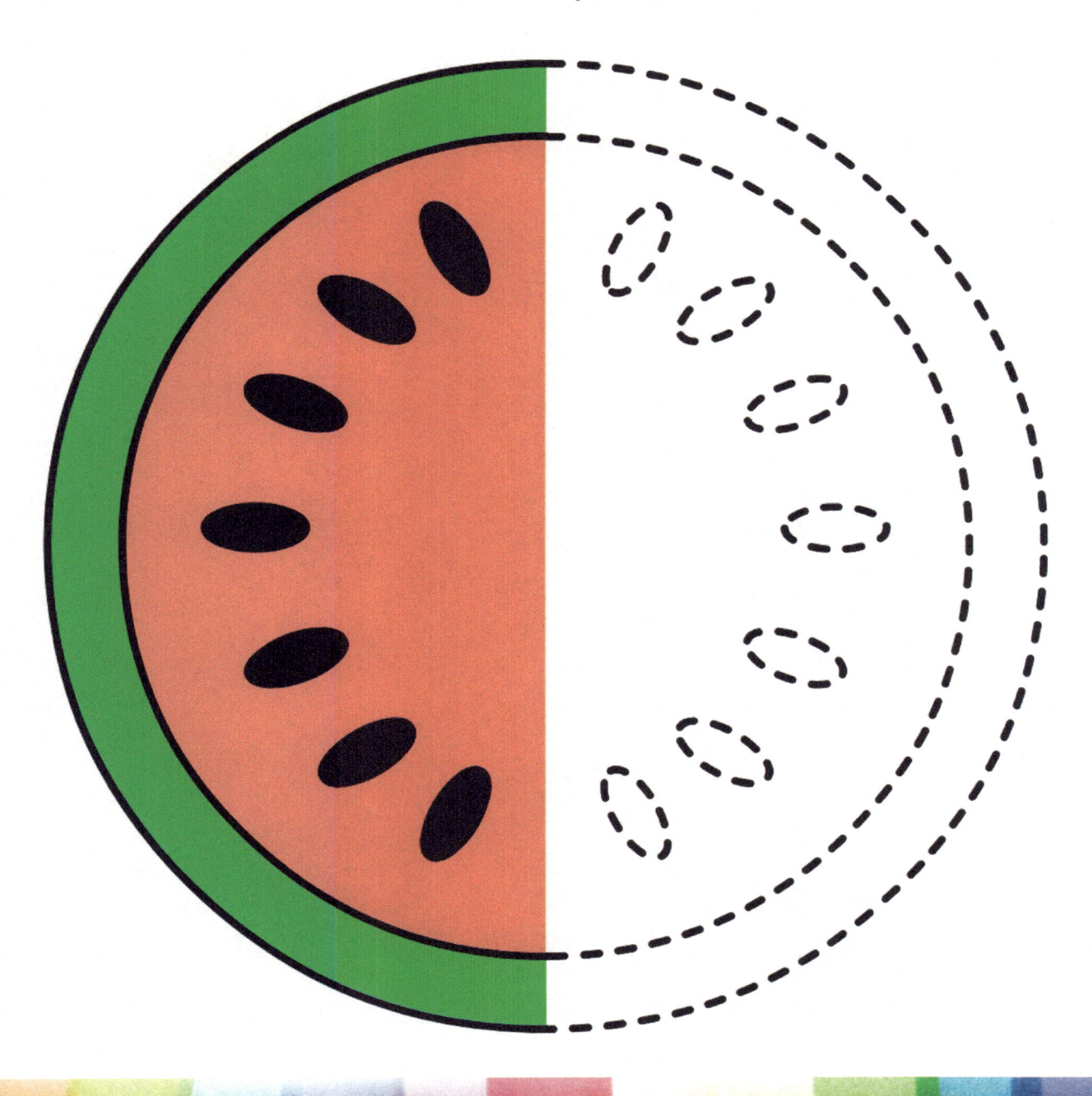

How Many Points?

Circle the correct number of points of each stars.

⭐ yellow star	4 / 5 / 6	🔶 orange sun	10 / 12 / 14
🟢 green star	8 / 9 / 11	🟠 orange star	6 / 7 / 8
🔵 blue star	6 / 8 / 10	🔷 teal star	5 / 6 / 7

ON THE LAND

DIRECTIONS: COLOR THE LAND ANIMALS BROWN.

AB PATTERNS

Complete the patterns by choosing the correct colour that comes next.

Create your own AB pattern.

CUT AND PASTE

cut and paste the objects to their matching shapes

This page intentionally blank

Dot-to-Dot

Connect the dots from 1 to 44, this way you practice counting and discover a cute animal.

NUMBER MATCHING

Circle the correct number to match the number.

Nine — 4 9 11

Eight — 6 8 9

Five — 5 6 15

Ten — 10 15 20

Eleven — 8 10 11

Twenty — 19 20 22

Twelve — 11 12 14

Sixteen — 15 16 19

Seventeen — 16 17 18

COUNTING 6-10
CUT AND PASTE ACTIVITY

Instructions: Count the scoops of ice cream. Match the scoops of ice cream to its corresponding cones.

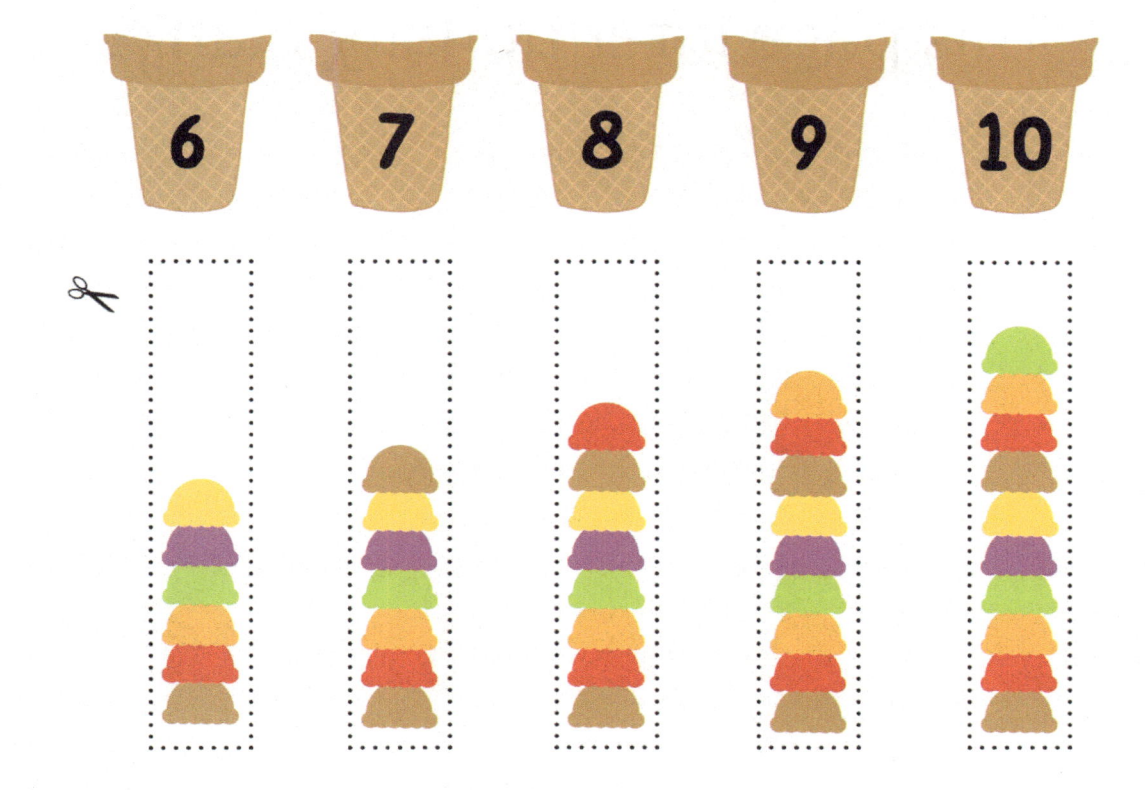

6 7 8 9 10

This page intentionally blank

How Many Sides?

Circle the correct number of sides of each shapes.

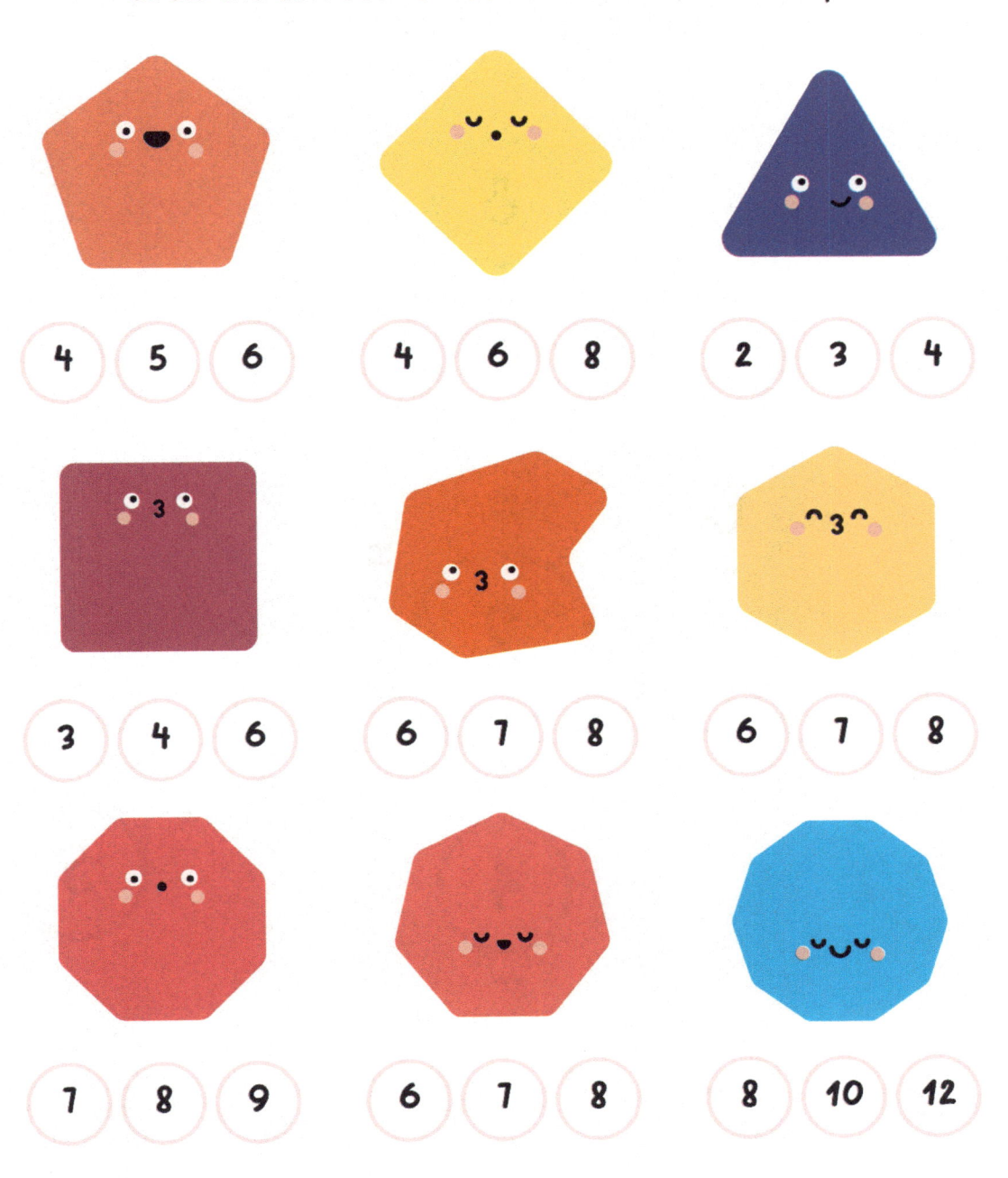

4 5 6   4 6 8   2 3 4

3 4 6   6 7 8   6 7 8

7 8 9   6 7 8   8 10 12

SUBTRACTION

Complete the Empty circles with the right numbers, so that the result of the subtraction is 2.

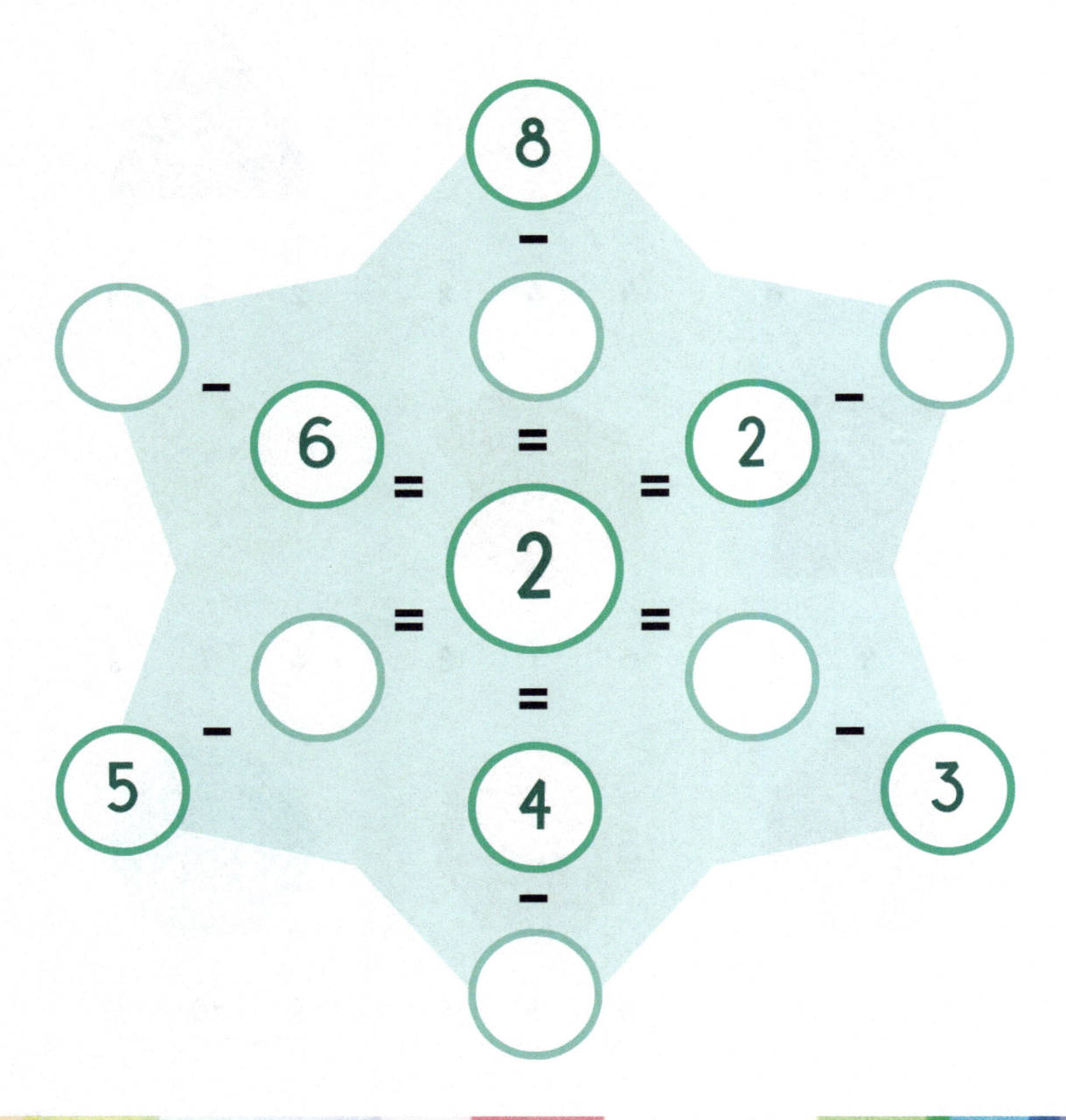

8 − ◯ = 6
◯ − 6 = 2
◯ − 4 = 2
4 − ◯ = 2
3 − ◯ = 2
◯ − 2 = 2
2 − ◯ = (cannot determine)

SMALLEST

Circle the smallest object in each row.

Shaped Pizza

- Count and color the shapes on the pizza.

1 2 3 4

Count to 100

Fill in the missing numbers and count to 100.
Enjoy this fun activity. Yes you can count!

1	2		4	5			8		10
11		13			16		18	19	
21	22		24		26	27		29	30
		33	34	35		37		39	
41	42			45		47	48		50
51		53	54	55	56			59	60
61	62	63		65		67			70
71		73	74		76		78		
	82	83		85	86	87	88		90
91			94	95		97		99	

Sweet Ollie

Sweet Ollie

Follow Sweet Ollie and explore their bibliography from Amazon.com's Sweet Ollie Author Page.

amazon.com

Made in the USA
Columbia, SC
21 October 2022